1980s Project Studies/Council on Foreign Relations

STUDIES AVAILABLE

SIX BILLION PEOPLE:
Demographic Dilemmas and World Politics
Studies by Georges Tapinos and Phyllis T. Piotrow

THE MIDDLE EAST IN THE COMING DECADE:
From Wellhead to Well-being?
Studies by John Waterbury and Ragaei El Mallakh

REDUCING GLOBAL INEQUITIES
Studies by W. Howard Wriggins and Gunnar Adler-Karlsson

RICH AND POOR NATIONS IN THE WORLD ECONOMY
Studies by Albert Fishlow, Carlos F. Díaz-Alejandro, Richard R. Fagen, and Roger D. Hansen

CONTROLLING FUTURE ARMS TRADE
Studies by Anne Hessing Cahn and Joseph J. Kruzel, by Peter M. Dawkins, and by Jacques Huntzinger

DIVERSITY AND DEVELOPMENT IN SOUTHEAST ASIA:
The Coming Decade
Studies by Guy J. Pauker, Frank H. Golay, and Cynthia H. Enloe

NUCLEAR WEAPONS AND WORLD POLITICS:
Alternatives for the Future
Studies by David C. Gompert, Michael Mandelbaum, Richard L. Garwin and John H. Barton

CHINA'S FUTURE:
Foreign Policy and Economic Development in the Post-Mao Era
Studies by Allen S. Whiting and by Robert F. Dernberger

ALTERNATIVES TO MONETARY DISORDER
Studies by Fred Hirsch and Michael W. Doyle and by Edward L. Morse

NUCLEAR PROLIFERATION:

Motivations, Capabilities, and Strategies for Control

Studies by Ted Greenwood and by Harold A. Feiveson and Theodore B. Taylor

INTERNATIONAL DISASTER RELIEF:

Toward a Responsive System

Stephen Green

STUDIES FORTHCOMING

The 1980s Project will comprise about 30 volumes. Most will contain independent but related studies concerning issues of potentially great importance in the next decade and beyond, such as resource management, human rights, population studies, and relations between the developing and developed societies, among many others. Additionally, a number of volumes will be devoted to particular regions of the world, concentrating especially on political and economic development trends outside the industrialized West.

Six Billion People

Six Billion People

DEMOGRAPHIC DILEMMAS AND WORLD POLITICS

GEORGES TAPINOS

PHYLLIS T. PIOTROW

Introduction by Edward L. Morse

1980s Project/Council on Foreign Relations

McGRAW-HILL BOOK COMPANY
New York   St. Louis   San Francisco
Auckland   Bogotá   Düsseldorf   Johannesburg   London   Madrid
Mexico   Montreal   New Delhi   Panama   São Paulo
Singapore   Sydney   Tokyo   Toronto

The Council on Foreign Relations, Inc., is a nonprofit and nonpartisan organization devoted to promoting improved understanding of international affairs through the free exchange of ideas. Its membership of about 1,700 persons throughout the United States is made up of individuals with special interest and experience in international affairs. The Council has no affiliation with and receives no funding from the United States government.

The Council publishes the quarterly journal *Foreign Affairs* and, from time to time, books and monographs that in the judgment of the Council's Committee on Studies are responsible treatments of significant international topics worthy of presentation to the public. The 1980s Project is a research effort of the Council; as such, 1980s Project Studies have been similarly reviewed through procedures of the Committee on Studies. As in the case of all Council publications, statements of fact and expressions of opinion contained in 1980s Project Studies are the sole responsibility of their authors.

The editor of this book was Abe Goldman for the Council on Foreign Relations. Thomas Quinn and Michael Hennelly were the editors for McGraw-Hill Book Company. Christopher Simon was the designer. Teresa Leaden supervised the production. This book was set in Times Roman by Creative Book Services, Inc.

Printed and bound by R. R. Donnelley & Sons.

Library of Congress Cataloging in Publication Data

Tapinos, Georges Photios.
Six billion people.

(1980s Project/Council on Foreign Relations)
Bibliography: p.
Includes index.
1. Population. 2. Population forecasting.
3. Population policy. I. Piotrow, Phyllis Tilson,
joint author. II. Title. III. Series: Council on
Foreign Relations. 1980s Project/Council on Foreign
Relations.
HB871.T26 1978   301.32   78-5775
ISBN 0-07-062876-9
ISBN 0-07-062877-7 pbk.

1 2 3 4 5 6 7 8 9 R R D R R D 7 8 3 2 1 0 9 8

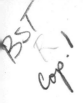

Contents

List of Tables

Foreword: The 1980s Project

These analyses of the future size and structure of the world's population and of the ways that population growth will affect other issues of public policy are part of a stream of studies being produced in the course of the 1980s Project of the Council on Foreign Relations. Each 1980s Project Study analyzes an issue or set of issues that is likely to be of international concern during the next 10 to 20 years.

The ambitious purpose of the 1980s Project is to examine important political and economic problems not only individually but in relationship to one another. Some studies or books produced by the Project will primarily emphasize the interrelationship of issues.. In the case of other, more specifically focused studies, a considerable effort has been made to write, review, and criticize them in the context of more general Project work. Each Project study is thus capable of standing on its own; at the same time it has been shaped by a broader perspective.

The 1980s Project had its origin in the widely held recognition that many of the assumptions, policies, and institutions that have characterized international relations during the past 30 years are inadequate to the demands of today and the foreseeable demands of the period between now and 1990 or so. Over the course of the next decade, substantial adaptation of institutions and behavior will be needed to respond to the changed circumstances of the 1980s and beyond. The Project seeks to identify those future conditions and the kinds of adaptation they might require. It is not the Project's purpose to arrive at a single or exclusive set of goals. Nor does it focus upon the foreign policy or national interests of the United States alone. Instead, it seeks to identify goals that are compatible with the perceived interests of most states, despite differences in ideology and in level of economic development.

The published products of the Project are aimed at a broad readership, including policy makers and potential policy makers and those who would influence the policy-making process, but are confined to no single nation or region. The authors of Project studies were therefore asked to remain mindful of interests broader than those of any one society and to take fully into account the likely realities of domestic politics in the principal societies involved. All those who have worked on the Project, however, have tried not to be captives of the status quo; they have sought to question the inevitability of existing patterns of thought and behavior that restrain desirable change and to look for ways in which those patterns might in time be altered or their consequences mitigated.

The 1980s Project is at once a series of separate attacks upon a number of urgent and potentially urgent international problems and also a collective effort, involving a substantial number of persons in the United States and abroad, to bring those separate approaches to bear upon one another and to suggest the kinds of choices that might be made among them. The Project involves more than 300 participants. A small central staff and a steering Coordinating Group have worked to define the questions and to assess the compatibility of policy prescriptions. Nearly 100 authors, from more than a dozen countries, have been at work on separate studies. Ten working groups of specialists and generalists have been convened to subject the Project's studies to critical scrutiny and to help in the process of identifying interrelationships among them.

The 1980s Project is the largest single research and studies effort the Council on Foreign Relations has undertaken in its 55-year history, comparable in conception only to a major study of the postwar world, the War and Peace Studies, undertaken by the Council during the Second World War. At that time, the impetus to the effort was the discontinuity caused by worldwide conflict and the visible and inescapable need to rethink, replace, and supplement many of the features of the international system that had prevailed before the war. The discontinuities in today's world are less obvious and, even when occasionally quite visible—as in the abandonment of gold convertibility and fixed monetary parities—only briefly command the spotlight of public attention. That new institutions and patterns of behavior are needed in many areas is widely acknowledged, but the sense of need is less urgent—existing institutions have not for the most part dramatically failed and collapsed. The tendency, therefore, is to make do with outmoded arrangements and to improvise rather than to undertake a basic analysis of the problems that lie before us and of the demands that those problems will place upon all nations.

The 1980s Project is based upon the belief that serious effort and integrated forethought can contribute—indeed, are indispensable—to progress in the next decade toward a more humane, peaceful, productive, and just world. And it rests upon the hope that participants in its deliberations and readers of Project publications—whether or not they agree with an author's point of view—may be helped to think more informedly about the opportunities and the dangers that lie ahead and the consequences of various possible courses of future action.

The 1980s Project has been made possible by generous grants from the Ford Foundation, the Lilly Endowment, the Andrew W. Mellon Foundation, the Rockefeller Foundation, and the German Marshall Fund of the United States. Neither the Council on Foreign Relations nor any of those foundations is responsible for statements of fact and expressions of opinion contained in publications of the 1980s Project; they are the sole responsibility of the individual authors under whose names they appear. But the Council on Foreign Relations and the staff of the 1980s Project take great pleasure in placing those publications before a wide readership both in the United States and abroad.

Edward L. Morse and Richard H. Ullman

xiii

1980s PROJECT WORKING GROUPS

During 1975 and 1976, ten Working Groups met to explore major international issues and to subject initial drafts of 1980s Project studies to critical review. Those who chaired Project Working Groups were:

Cyrus R. Vance, Working Group on Nuclear Weapons and Other Weapons of Mass Destruction

Leslie H. Gelb, Working Group on Armed Conflict

Roger Fisher, Working Group on Transnational Violence and Subversion

Rev. Theodore M. Hesburgh, Working Group on Human Rights

Joseph S. Nye, Jr., Working Group on the Political Economy of North-South Relations

Harold Van B. Cleveland, Working Group on Macroeconomic Policies and International Monetary Relations

Lawrence C. McQuade, Working Group on Principles of International Trade

William Diebold, Jr., Working Group on Multinational Enterprises

Eugene B. Skolnikoff, Working Group on the Environment, the Global Commons, and Economic Growth

Miriam Camps, Working Group on Industrial Policy

1980s PROJECT STAFF

Persons who have held senior professional positions on the staff of the 1980s Project for all or part of its duration are:

Miriam Camps	*Catherine Gwin*
William Diebold, Jr.	*Roger D. Hansen*
Tom J. Farer	*Edward L. Morse*
David C. Gompert	*Richard H. Ullman*

Richard H. Ullman was Director of the 1980s Project from its inception in 1974 until July 1977, when he became Chairman of the Project Coordinating Group. At that time, Edward L. Morse became Executive Director of the Project.

PROJECT COORDINATING GROUP

The Coordinating Group of the 1980s Project had a central advisory role in the work of the Project. Its members as of December 31, 1976, were:

W. Michael Blumenthal
Richard N. Cooper
Carlos F. Díaz-Alejandro
Richard A. Falk
Tom J. Farer
Edward K. Hamilton
Stanley Hoffmann
Samuel P. Huntington
Gordon J. MacDonald
Bruce K. MacLaury

Bayless Manning
Theodore R. Marmor
Ali Mazrui
Joseph S. Nye, Jr.
Michael O'Neill
Marshall D. Shulman
Stephen Stamas
Fritz Stern
Allen S. Whiting

COMMITTEE ON STUDIES

The Committee on Studies of the Board of Directors of the Council on Foreign Relations is the governing body of the 1980s Project. The Committee's members as of December 31, 1976, were:

W. Michael Blumenthal
Zbigniew Brzezinski
Robert A. Charpie
Richard N. Cooper

Walter J. Levy
Joseph S. Nye, Jr.
Robert V. Roosa
Carroll L. Wilson

James A. Perkins (Chairman)

Six Billion People

Population and World Politics

Edward L. Morse

Curbing world population growth is a central issue on virtually every list of major international problems existing during the remainder of this century and well into the next. It is the exemplary issue of all arguments that traditional international politics are being challenged by new concerns about the quality of human life and reduced emphasis on the security of national communities. For population growth has been responsible for the recognition that an intolerable gap in living standards between the richest and poorest people of the world must be overcome and that living conditions must be made more equitable around the globe. The issue of population growth, in short, is the primary reason for and illustration of the global nature of today's politics.

Controlling world population is clearly the first requirement of a moderate, just, and equitable international order. Control of population growth is essential for making any progress to alleviate the conditions of absolute poverty in which a billion or so persons now live and in which many more could well live by the end of this century. Malnutrition, poor housing, illiteracy, lack of water, and inadequate sanitation facilities present a challenge of such enormity that reducing fertility, especially in the developing world, is of interest to all societies. Inexorable population growth—regardless of how quickly reproduction rates are reduced—will be a primary factor in creating conditions of unemployment on an unprecedented scale throughout most of the developing world, and will thereby create political instability and environments ripe for political revolution, which can affect global security. Unless population growth is curbed, moreover, efforts to come to grips with its attendant political problems will more likely than not result in the imposition by governments of stringent controls over population movements—limiting entry into urban areas—as a means of maintaining political order and experimenting with new modes and strategies of economic growth. Population growth clearly affects the political and moral climate of the entire international system.

The international scope of the burgeoning population problem is dramatically illustrated in instances where developed and developing countries share contiguous boundaries, which will be permeable to the illegal international migration of persons from poorer societies seeking better conditions for themselves and their children among their richer neighbors. Nor will illegal immigration be avoided in developed countries that, while not contiguous with less developed countries (LDCs), are sufficiently close that illegal international migration will prove to be an irresistible temptation. Profound policy dilemmas will be confronted, especially in the industrialized world, as governments try to impede illegal migration over the course of the next two decades. Policy choices will include efforts to export capital to neighboring developing societies to assure that employment opportunities in them expand as a means of curbing transnational migration, and unless domestic employment conditions in the industrialized world radically improve, such efforts to "export jobs" will by no means prove easy.

Because different ethnic groups will experience different population-growth rates over the next decade, and because these groups more often than not live in two or more states—especially in developing areas such as Africa—new international security issues will arise as a result of population growth and the ethnic conflicts it will feed into. The causes of these conflicts will obviously be diverse. They will include efforts of some national groups, as in the recent case of the Somalis in the African Horn, to forge a nation out of ethnically affiliated people who live in more than one nation-state. But they will also include armed conflicts within states, between those groups whose traditional exercise of power is challenged and oppressed or disenfranchised minorities or majorities whose numbers are increasing at faster rates. Ethnic conflicts over resources and over control of government will be instigated both by those wishing to conserve power and by those hoping to gain access to it. However they occur, these conflicts will challenge the ability of regional and global institutions to develop means to mediate, establish truces, and peacefully resolve conflicts.

Population growth, finally, will create increasingly numerous and more profound efforts to deal with what will be perceived as common problems. They will be common in two senses. First, growth in population will rapidly increase demands on resources for which governments and people compete internationally: for food, for the raw materials of industrial growth, for capital and technology, for markets that will secure jobs for those who work in export industries. Second, they will be common in the sense that they will affect different national communities in similar ways. Problems of urban environments—for example, housing, transportation, sanitation—will not resemble the problems of common ocean space, in which overuse by some restricts access of others to fishing, navigation, and mineral resources. Rather, they will be common in the sense that experiments undertaken in some areas will be of interest to others in different national political communities undertaking to solve similar problems.

Both sorts of common problems have already appeared on the agendas of major international institutions, including the United Nations, with its conferences in 1971 on the environment, in 1974 on food and on population, and in 1976 on habitat. They will likely tax the capacities of existing international institutions to such a degree that their successful resolution will require not only the reform of these institutions but also, perhaps, even wholesale restructuring and international institutional innovation.

The issues raised by population growth, in short, cut across all others in the 1980s Project, for which the three essays that appear in this volume were commissioned. The effects of population growth are ubiquitous. They are momentous in their implications for the way the international community is organized. Indeed, they are central to determining whether it will be possible

3

to devise ground rules on international affairs so that a moderate and just international order can be created.

The first essay, by Georges Tapinos of the Institut National d'Études Démographiques and the Institut d'Études Politiques in Paris, describes the expected evolution of the world's population for the remainder of this century and outlines some of the main challenges to population policy: urbanization, the economic costs of demographic change, ethnic conflict, internal and international migration, and the geopolitical balance among states. Phyllis T. Piotrow, executive director of the Population Crisis Committee, analyzes the success of fertility policies during the past two decades and argues, in the second essay in this volume, that fertility will be reduced to manageable levels by the end of this century. However, problems of social control of unprecedented proportions will emerge as the central issues of population policy. In the final essay, Georges Tapinos provides a critical examination of the major existing demographic projections and evaluates the confidence that public officials should place in them.

The three essays in this volume leave no doubt that population growth will play an increasingly important and central role in world affairs. Of course, few people have ever doubted that demographic factors are important in international politics. But as these essays also illustrate, it is unclear exactly what kind of role these factors play and what sorts of policies are needed for the world to cope with and manage the effects of historically unprecedented levels of population growth.

To be sure, there are some schools of thought that claim to take into account the implications of population growth. Today population growth is a central focus of popularized Malthusian scenarios concerning presumed scarcities that, in the minds of their publicists, are likely to characterize tomorrow's world. This focus contrasts sharply with pronatalist policies that governments once pursued in the belief that vigorous population growth was a symbol of national strength and a requisite of international power. As the essays in this volume forcefully argue, a decade from now neither Malthusian nor Darwinian perspectives will dominate thinking about population. Instead, a variety of new

4

and intransigent domestic and international problems will derive from conditions related to population.

Fertility Policies

Attitudes toward demographic conditions are difficult to translate into appropriate policy responses. For the past generation, fertility control has been considered a central factor for fostering economic and political development. Aid donors and philanthropic organizations, in particular, raised consciousness about the need to reduce birthrates, especially in developing countries, as a necessary means of accelerating economic development and raising standards of living. Yet aid-recipient countries have been strikingly unwilling to make the reduction of fertility a priority issue. The short-term perspective of governments leads them to focus on more immediate concerns than the size of their populations a generation or so in the future. Fertility control, at any rate, frequently requires governments actively to transform fundamental social and religious attitudes toward procreation, and the active effort to do so often leads to a weakening of governmental authority and legitimacy in the eyes of too many social groups. In developing countries, whose governments are concerned with staying in office and building up domestic political support, the political risks entailed in vigorous efforts to curtail fertility are simply too great.

Impeding the battle against population growth as well has been the view that there is little one can do about it anyway. As Georges Tapinos argues in the third essay in this volume, demographic theory is weakest in its analysis of conditions that affect fertility. And reinforcing this reluctance by many governments in the less developed world to do little more than voice concern over fertility levels has been the undertone of outside intervention by rich countries in poorer ones. The concern manifested for fertility control in the developed world clearly smacks of interference in the internal affairs of the developing countries. And as some developing-country representatives have argued, especially at the UN conference in Bucharest in 1974, the focus on fertility control can be seen as an excuse by rich societies for not dealing with what the LDCs see as the major requirements of economic development: increases in transfers of income and technology and changes in international trading rules to facilitate exports of semiprocessed and industrial goods from poorer societies to richer ones.

In spite of the politicization of fertility policies, there is growing evidence that the corner has been turned in reducing the high fertility levels of developing countries. Phyllis Piotrow documents, in her essay in this volume, the growing number of developing countries whose governments have quietly implemented birth control programs, often in contradiction to the public positions they take on population issues. As well, she makes it clear that great changes have taken place throughout the world in attitudes toward family planning. Societies almost everywhere are far more receptive now than ever before to the desirability of curbing birthrates and reducing the average size of families, whether or not this change in attitudes can be attributed to family-planning programs.

No one challenges the need to continue efforts to reduce fertility levels in the developing areas of the world. While trends now seem to indicate what Dr. Piotrow terms "substantial declines in fertility"—from birthrates of roughly the level of 40 per thousand to 35 per thousand—the time is not yet in sight when birthrates will be equalized across industrial and developing societies, let alone when more manageable increases in absolute numbers will take place. Thus, efforts to reduce fertility will remain important for the rest of this century. Even if fertility is in the process of being controlled, 900 million adults in the developing world will be in their peak reproductive years—15 to 30—in 1990. And it is by no means clear that voluntary family-planning services—even those supported by governments—will be capable of meeting this generation's needs. Even if voluntary sterilization, abortions, and various older as well as newer contraceptive devices become widespread as the model of a smaller family becomes more acceptable, still more will be required. Thus, even if one is as optimistic as Phyllis Piotrow tends to be that much progress will be made during the next decade in the organization and delivery of family-planning services, there remains scope for much more to be done.

6

One alternative—or supplement—to voluntary services is, of course, governmental coercion of the sort practiced in China for the past two and one-half decades and in India in the mid-1970s. But social, cultural and religious values throughout most of Latin America and Africa will make it unlikely that coercion or other governmental pressures will be acceptable instruments of family planning. Only in Asia will it be feasible for governments to move beyond voluntary services. But, as Phyllis Piotrow reminds us, "In the long run, in the developing countries as elsewhere, the most effective and acceptable forms of pressure on individuals to reduce fertility will come from the most immediate sources, from community or even family leaders who can identify and articulate a community or personal need better than the more remote national government."[1] And in the short run, it is likely that fertility control policies fostered by governments will be justified not by demographic reasoning but rather by other political objectives: improvement of the status of women, more equitable income distribution, compulsory education, improved health, old-age security, etc. However, the upshot is still clear: reducing fertility will be almost universally accepted as a national goal a decade from now.

Despite the obvious fact that policies to control fertility will be carried out by and large on a national basis, there also is considerable scope for improving the role played by international agencies. Phyllis Piotrow identifies four areas in which international roles will remain important and in which more efficient and larger programs could be justified: assistance to the poorest groups in developing countries for extending services, training, and popular education for family planning and contraception; research into contraceptive techniques; support for social science research in developing countries on the relationship between demographic factors and development planning; and raising of global consciousness about the importance of curbing demographic growth in order to enhance other economic and social goals.

It is hard to understate pressures that governments—especially in the developing world—will have to confront as a result of the

[1]See below, p. 135.

7

magnitudes involved in population increases. The world's population, which was about 3 billion in 1960, reached 4 billion by the mid-1970s and will exceed 5 billion by 1990, regardless of how effective fertility control policies may be. Depending upon how rapidly fertility rates fall and when a targetted net reproduction rate of 1.0 is achieved, the world's population will likely be stabilized somewhere between 8 and 14 billion by the end of the next century. The difference between these two estimates—6 billion persons—is enormous, representing twice the total population of the world two decades ago. The fact that this range exists means that it is urgent to continue to tackle the problem of fertility control on a global basis. As Robert S. McNamara, President of the International Bank for Reconstruction and Development (IBRD), made clear in a speech at MIT in 1977, international institutions, including the IBRD, must strive both directly and indirectly to implement policies to normalize the small-size family. But whether net reproduction rates of 1.0 are reached in 2000 or 2020 or 2030 will not affect other extraordinary problems that will have to be confronted by the end of this century.

The main problems imposed by population growth are, of course, outside the special competence of demographers. They relate to political problems of social control, domestic strategies for economic growth, international industrial policies, international security, and the structure and operations of international institutions. These wider issues are discussed in the essays in this volume. While the importance of these issues is noted, the authors can offer little more than general prescriptions about them. It might prove helpful to summarize briefly a few of these major issues related to population growth and their wider implications for international society over the course of the next two decades. Many of the issues are the focus of other studies that will appear in companion volumes in the 1980s Project series.

Absolute Poverty and Basic Human Needs

The most intractable of all issues raised by population growth is the increase in the number of poor persons living in absolute poverty, below the subsistence level. Regardless of how effective

8

efforts might be to reduce birthrates between now and 1990, total world population will reach 5.3 billion persons, 4 billion of whom will live in developing countries—about the same as the total number of persons alive in 1976. Rough estimates indicate that about 40 percent of people in the developing world—about 1 billion of the 2.5 billion who lived there in 1970—live beneath what Mahbub ul Haq calls "the Poverty Curtain."[2] These are persons whose nutrition, housing and sanitation facilities, water and food supplies, and educational levels are below minimal standards of life. And they are the same persons whose birthrates are at the highest levels. Unless efforts are made now to deal with absolute poverty, it could well be that the total number of persons living in inhumane conditions could exceed 1.6 billion by 1990, even if great strides are made in economic growth over the next 10 years.[3]

Decades of experience with economic development have proven that this lowest 40 percent of the populations of developing countries is the most difficult group to reach via a "trickle-down" process of growth. Moreover, the enormous magnitude of the problem of absolute poverty suggests that it can be dealt with only by a direct attack. Recognition that this is the case has been growing in the aid community as well as among intellectuals from the developing world.[4] And many international aid-giving institutions are now gearing themselves up to deal with a global approach to the poverty issue.

The rationales for dealing with absolute poverty are moral, prudential, political, and economic. The first three relate to the intolerability of a growing gap between the richest and poorest people in the world. A world that is knit increasingly closer by modern communications and by material interdependences can-

[2]Mahbub ul Haq, *The Poverty Curtain: Choices for the Third World*, Columbia University Press, New York, 1976.

[3]For a fuller discussion of these issues, see another 1980s Project study: W. Howard Wriggins and Gunnar Adler-Karlsson, *Reducing Global Inequities*, McGraw-Hill Book Company for the Council on Foreign Relations, New York, 1978.

[4]See, for example, *The Assault on World Poverty*, Johns Hopkins University Press for the World Bank, Baltimore, 1975; and Jan Tinbergen (coordinator), *Reshaping the International Order: A Report to the Club of Rome*, E. P. Dutton, New York, 1976.

not justify this gap on moral grounds. Political instabilities that are likely to accompany the growth in conditions of absolute poverty make it wise on prudential grounds to do something about it. Politically, it seems clear that aid from richer industrialized societies to poorer ones, aimed at basic needs, can be used as a bargaining device to modify the intransigence of LDCs on many international issues: law of the seas, trade, finance, energy, and other issues in the North-South dialogue.

Economic arguments are, perhaps, even more compelling. Despite the uncertainties surrounding knowledge about what affects fertility and how it is affected, Georges Tapinos's second essay below makes it clear that fertility is broadly correlated with socioeconomic conditions: literacy, nutrition, and economic opportunities for personal advancement. Basic education, as well as education about birth control, lower infant mortality due to better health education and services, and alternatives for personal fulfillment and financial improvement for both women and men are inducements for reducing the birthrate in a society. It may well be the case, in short, that for purposes of economic development, the vicious circle of high fertility and poverty must be broken. And while one short-term effect of improvements in housing, nutrition, and sanitation will certainly be reduced infant mortality and, therefore, higher rates of population growth, in the long run this seems to be the best course of action to take to reduce fertility.

Moreover, there is impressive evidence that, during the past two decades, while the upper tier of developing countries has sustained a remarkably high annual growth rate of more than 6.5 percent, it has done so at the expense of equitable domestic income distribution. The gap between rich and poor in poor societies—like the gap between North and South in the international system—has grown in spite of phenomenal economic growth in many cases.[5] Not only is a direct approach to absolute poverty required as part of an effort to make economic growth

[5]See Hollis Chenery et al., *Redistribution with Growth*, Oxford University Press for the World Bank and the Institute of Development Studies at University of Sussex, London, 1974; and Charles R. Frank, Jr. and Richard C. Webb (eds.), *Income Distribution and Growth in the Less-Developed Countries*, The Brookings Institution, Washington, D.C. 1977.

more effective—by enabling more people to benefit from growth—but also an effort is needed to reduce the perverse effects of growth on the impoverishment of displaced individuals and to enable growth to take place on a more equitable basis.

Thus, the broad general relationship between economic growth and population growth suggests that in the long run the best means of curbing fertility is through economic development. And in the short run, major issues of population policy will be in the pursuit of fulfilling basic human needs in developing countries. In both short-term and long-term perspectives, these fundamental issues raised by population growth require less the attention of demographers than of specialists in economic development and of institutions responsible for economic assistance.

Unemployment, Urbanization, Development Strategies, and Human Rights

What Phyllis Piotrow calls a "new, more populous, and more volatile" young generation of rootless and unemployed individuals in the developing world requires not simply policies to deal with absolute poverty but a range of other policies as well. Unless these latter policies can be implemented, population growth will be a threat to political—and more generally to social—stability in a number of developing countries. What will be required are major efforts to deal with an unprecedented rate of unemployment. What will likely occur is an unprecedented range of policies of social control, raising significant questions of human rights. Of central importance is the question of whether governments will successfully be able to curtail internal movement of persons by offering them in return adequate employment opportunities.

These problems stem from a demographic condition that cannot be dealt with through curbing fertility. During the next 15 years, almost 1 billion persons already born in developing countries will be between 15 and 30 years old. This flood of energetic individuals will pose major problems for governments, related to their needs and demands for adequate housing, employment, and education and their likely desire to migrate away from overcrowded rural areas to urban centers in the quest for new opportunities. And as Phyllis Piotrow argues, in coping with this

11

human flood governments will likely pursue a mix of five basic strategies, some of which contradict others: rapid urbanization, agricultural modernization, integrated rural development, dispersed urbanization, and regional development. But a major requirement will probably be a new focus on development strategy, which centers on integrated rural development based less on agricultural "modernization" than on an appropriate means of maintaining an efficient but labor-intensive agricultural sector.

A central objective of rural development will inevitably be increased productivity for rural smallholders, to meet the dual need to secure rural employment opportunities and food for a growing population. This focus of integrated strategies for rural development is part of newer development strategies whose emphasis is oriented toward employment opportunities in urban as well as rural areas.[6] Among the features of some of these strategies, however, are efforts to decentralize manufacturing activities, when appropriate, by locating new plants in rural areas to provide adequate job opportunities for rural workers and reduce migration toward urban centers.[7]

The upshot, in short, is likely to be a great deal of experimentation with new growth strategies oriented to meet employment needs as well as growth targets. Experimentation will be required because the conditions that made integrated rural development strategies—land reform and decentralization of production—appropriate for Taiwan and South Korea are not necessarily replicable elsewhere in the developing world. In some instances, it might be appropriate to rely on more traditional growth strategies, focusing on export-sector manufacturing in urban settings, where growth might have its traditional impact of job creation. But regardless of the pattern followed in a particular LDC, major obstacles will impede success—usually because the problems of unemployment will be beyond the capacity of governments to resolve. Governments will need exceptional powers to marshal domestic support for such strategies.

[6]See, for example, the report of the International Labor Organization, *Employment, Growth and Basic Needs: A One-World Problem*, International Labour Organization, Geneva, 1976.

[7]See John W. Mellor, *The New Economics of Growth*, Cornell University Press, Ithaca, N.Y. 1976.

International Migration and Industrial Policy

There is an obvious, but limited, role that the international community can play in helping LDCs to implement policies to deal with absolute poverty or new, employment-oriented development strategies. To be sure, reorientation of lending and aid policies through such international agencies as the World Bank or the UN Development Program can help governments to deal with these issues. Although the main burdens will inevitably be carried by national governments in domestic settings, the same population pressures that now are giving rise to employment-oriented development strategies will likely pose major international problems a decade or so from now. Indeed, they already are posing problems.

Unemployment and the search for a better way of life by persons in the developing world will create increasing incentives for migration not only from the rural countryside to urban centers but also from the developing world to industrialized countries—especially in Western Europe and North America. And international migration will involve skilled and professional middle-class people—such as doctors and scientists—as well as unskilled and semiskilled persons.

International migration has, of course, been much easier for governments to control than has national migration. Indeed, strict control of the international movement of people has been in effect for almost a century, since for nationalistic and racial reasons, governments first began to impose restrictions on immigration and to distinguish between "desirable" and "undesirable" immigrants. But the openness of Western industrialized societies, the difficulties for their governments of imposing strict border controls, and the low cost of international transportation will tempt increasing numbers of persons to migrate illegally in search of a better way of life.

As Georges Tapinos argues in the first study in this volume, a new wave of international migration is already under way and is comparable in scale to the great transoceanic migration of the turn of the century. There is no escape from the conclusion that this wave will continue, especially from Mediterranean Europe to Northern Europe, from Africa to Western Europe, and from

Mexico, Central America, and the Caribbean to the United States. And population pressures will largely be behind this movement. As Georges Tapinos argues, potentially large pressures will occur if, for example, the United States population grows at low rates between now and the next century and Mexico's grows at high rates. Whereas Mexico's population was almost one-third the size of the United States population in 1975 (59 versus 213 million persons), by 1995/2000 Mexico's could well grow to be more than one-half America's (140 versus 250 million persons).

Illegal migration into advanced industrialized societies will obviously pose many dilemmas, especially for governments in the North. The pool of semiskilled and unskilled labor will certainly increase as a result, benefiting industrialized societies whose own populations have been decreasingly willing to assume "demeaning" positions. But almost all industrialized societies today are suffering from severe problems of unemployment. Illegal immigrants, who often accept low-wage jobs, are regarded as threats to native workers since they can reduce further the employment opportunities of citizens and legal-alien residents. Moreover, their presence in industrialized societies can create severe social costs: welfare system benefits and other direct costs and the multiple indirect costs associated with the socialization of persons whose language, cultural traits, and race differ from these of the majority of the larger community.

Human rights issues are raised here as well. What rights should be granted to an increasingly large reserve of legal-alien residents in industrialized societies? Should they be able to obtain the same social benefits as citizens? This issue has been raised recently in Europe when, with the deep recession of the mid-1970s, alien workers tended to be among the first to be laid off their jobs. Under such circumstances, should they be entitled to unemployment benefits and access to retraining programs on an equal footing with citizens? Should they be enfranchised under certain circumstances—for example, for voting on local political issues when, in some cases, they form the majority or near majority of a local constituency? Or should they have no say at all over these issues, even if their taxes contribute significantly to housing, education, and other social service programs?

One means of reducing the scale of legal as well as illegal international migration is the creation of employment opportunities in those developing countries from which the alien workers will tend to come. Capital investments by governments or multinational firms in these developing areas could, by fostering employment, make it more attractive for workers to stay in their native countries. Large-scale and rationalized investment programs, which mobilize capital and direct international flows, imply the need for a more structured and self-conscious industrial policy program that would be truly international. But international industrial policy also involves dilemmas and difficult choices for all parties.[8]

Developing countries would have to make the terms of investment attractive in order to gain sustained foreign investment. But attractive investment terms could also suggest a loss of control over domestic economic activity. Even carefully worked out terms of equity relationships between foreign and national participants could, for political reasons, become sources of friction. For in case of domestic political strife, governments will continue to be tempted to focus upon foreign investors as targets of attack if, in a short-term perspective, the governments feel they can thereby mobilize domestic political support for their own programs. Similar dilemmas will confront the governments of industrialized countries, especially if in the coming decade or so these societies continue to be plagued by chronic problems of unemployment. Not only will pressures exist to restrict imports from those developing countries whose export industries could threaten markets in industrialized countries while providing domestic employment opportunities for themselves, but also interest groups in industrial societies will continue to lobby to restrict the export of capital in order to channel domestic investments into new industries at home.

The upshot will be difficulties in working out international industrial policies, whether they are structured along bilateral lines—for example, between the United States and Mexico—or on a multilateral basis—for example, between the European community and its associates in the Mediterranean basin. But

[8]The subject of international industrial policy and its attendant problems are discussed in a forthcoming 1980s Project study by William Diebold, Jr.

whatever difficulties might be confronted, there is little likely escape from more coherent efforts at international industrial policies in the years ahead.

Ethnic and Other International Conflicts

Differential population growth rates between neighboring national communities and between ethnic groups in the same or neighboring societies will result in domestic and international conflagrations over the next decade or so. This is all the more likely to be the case since differential population growth among groups striving for greater control over economic and political resources heightens ethnic self-consciousness and serves to upset political bargains between groups worked out in earlier periods of time.

Georges Tapinos's analysis of differential demographic growth rates between a series of neighboring and potential (or actual) adversaries is highly suggestive of the likelihood of future international conflicts emerging from shifting international balances. United States–Mexican, West European–North African, Israeli–Arab, Chinese–Indian, and Turkish–Greek relations, among others, will be affected by differential population growth rates, which could widen the options of some governments and decrease those of others. Obviously, it is difficult to weigh the precise role that population growth will play in such conflicts. National power and international balances are determined by many elements other than population, and large populations undergoing high growth rates can create weakness far more than strength. But the major point is that both national perceptions of power and actual international balances will continue to be affected significantly by population growth.

More worrisome in the middle term are cases of internal conflicts due to ethnic rivalry and their potential for spillover into the international arena.[9]

[9]These conflicts are the subject of several 1980s Project studies. See, for example, Guy J. Pauker, Frank H. Golay, and Cynthia Enloe, *Diversity and Development in Southeast Asia*, McGraw-Hill Book Company for the Council on Foreign Relations, New York, 1977; and forthcoming 1980s Project regional studies on Africa, South Asia, Latin America, and Eastern Europe.

Domestic conflict in Lebanon during the past decade may exemplify future ethnic disputes in the Middle East, Africa, Southeast Asia, Eastern Europe, and even the Soviet Union in coming decades. In Lebanon, a political constitution that reflected the demographic balance between Moslem and Christian communities in the early 1940s was torn apart 30 years later when the accumulated effects of higher Moslem birthrates—42 per thousand versus 25 per thousand for Christians—made the majoritarian Moslems feel deprived of their rightful political and economic position. And since the interests of Palestinian immigrants also fed into domestic strife in Lebanon, local internal conflict quickly became internationalized and embroiled in intra-Arab disputes as well as the wider Arab-Israeli conflict.

Other ethnic disputes will be internationalized less because what is at issue within one society can affect regional balances and more because ethnic groups are divided into contiguous or neighboring states. The Kurds in the Middle East, the Somalis in East Africa, and a myriad of ethnic groups throughout the African and Asian continents make the probability of international conflicts over ethnicity, group autonomy, or more mundane power politics a virtual certainty in the decades ahead.

The outbreak of ethnic conflict could also tax the ability of neighboring societies, regional institutions, and the UN system in efforts to isolate violence and peacefully resolve disputes. Indeed, the likelihood of interethnic violence on an international level is going to challenge the imagination of regional institutions and the UN in devising new procedures and practices for mediation and even peacekeeping. Few instances of interethnic conflict will be amenable to the kinds of peacekeeping actions undertaken by the Syrian government in Lebanon in the 1970s. In most instances no such outside agency will exist, or if one does, it will not be welcomed by the disputing parties.

New efforts at peacekeeping, mediation, and dispute settlement will, of course, require a fundamental change in attitudes within international institutions as well as within and among societies prone to undergo such violence. Ethnic problems in most developing countries will be regarded by governments as purely internal matters, and outside intervention will be seen as reminiscent of colonial days. But working in the other direction will be many incentives, including the desire to restrict the actions of superpower intervenors or the potential intervention of larger regional powers, which will prompt nations to turn to international agencies in some instances as an acceptable alternative. Whether international institutions will be capable of generating the imaginative policy responses likely to be required remains for the time being an open question.

More vexing still are the problems of group conflict within some societies in instances where the international effects will likely be only indirect. There are vast latent conflicts of this sort throughout the industrialized world, including Ulster, Belgium, Yugoslavia, and the Soviet Union, where the Russian population is becoming increasingly minoritarian and where ethnic-group antipathy to Russian dominance could increasingly lead to violence. In many instances, conflict has been more open than latent. In most instances of this sort, there is little scope for international action to stop the outbreak of conflict, but the potential international effects of conflict could be rather great indeed.

* * * * * * * * * * * * *

There is no escape from the need to deal with a wide range of virtually ubiquitous problems related to unprecedented population growth. Ironically, as the three essays in this volume make clear, the areas of direct concern to population specialists, such as reducing infant mortality and curbing fertility, are decreasingly relevant to the problems that will be posed by demographic growth in the coming decades. Rather, these newer problems will relate to urban growth, international migration, social control, trade, and international investment. The essays in this volume do not prescribe ways to handle these newer issues. But they make the necessary and preliminary step of identifying areas to which population-policy analysis and policy making will shift in the coming years.

The World in the 1980s: Demographic Perspectives

Georges Tapinos

ONE

The Demographic Situation, 1970-1990

OVERVIEW

Demographic projections evoke curiosity, obsession, and hope. Futurology is the domain of science fiction and utopia, but also of demography; human beings are curious about their future, and any calculation about it, even one filled with reservations, is usually taken seriously by the public. In fact, ever since Malthus developed his influential theory on the tension between geometrically increasing population and arithmetically increasing resources, the irresistible growth of population has become an obsession. But demographic projections also raise certain hopes that the future can be controlled, and those hopes will play a part in molding the world in the 1980s. Although the projections on which they are based, like the products of any other science devised by human beings, are bound to be imperfect, they will

Note: This essay and the last essay in this volume were translated from the original French by Edward L. Morse. The author wishes to thank Messrs. Kono (UN Population Division), J. C. Chesnais, G. Galot, and H. Le Bras (Institut National d'Etudes Demographiques) for their valuable comments on an earlier draft.

Figures used in this section are based on the results of the most recent projections for the period 1970–2000. They come primarily from the following sources: United Nations, Department of Economic and Social Affairs, Population Division, *World Population Prospects as Assessed in 1973*, New York, 1977 (ST/ESA/Ser. A 60); United Nations, Department of Economic and Social Affairs, Population Division, *Selected World Demographic Indicators by Countries, 1950–2000*, working paper no. 55, New York, May 28, 1975.

nevertheless serve as the foundation of efforts in the 1980s to develop an ideal but feasible world order.

Virtually every aspect of international relations will be affected, either directly or indirectly, by the explosive growth and change in structure of the world's population in the period 1970–1990. The policy implications of population growth will confront public authorities around the world regardless of what efforts may be made to curb such growth in the short run. In this essay, some major international policy questions relating directly to demographic growth will be outlined, and by way of background the evolution of the world's population during the period 1970–1990 will be summarized. The essay begins with a summary of major existing projections of the world's population, both on a general basis and for specifically selected regional areas. Distinctions are made between what is likely to happen in the developed areas and emerging patterns in the less developed parts of the world. The essay concludes with a description of some major issues relating to population growth that are likely to become salient items on the international diplomatic agenda: the effects of changes in population structures on pension costs, education systems, and housing; the relationships between ethnic groups within and among societies as differential growth rates between groups affect political tensions; legal and illegal migration from poorer to richer societies as people try to improve their access to greater material well-being; and, finally, the geopolitical balances among nations.

SOME DEMOGRAPHIC TERMINOLOGY

Since this essay and the last essay in this volume make use of some technical demographic terminology, the following definitions will be helpful:

Dependency ratio: According to the UN, the number of people under 15 and over 65 in relation to every 1,000 members of the population who are aged 15 to 64. This ratio is considered an indicator of the economically active segment of the population.

Crude birthrate: The ratio of number of births occurring during a year to the average population of that year (per 1,000).

Crude death rate: The ratio of number of deaths occurring during a year to the average population of that year (per 1,000).

Natural increase rate: The difference between the crude birthrate and the crude death rate.

Growth rate: A comparison of the size of the total population at the beginning and end of a given period. It is expressed as a percentage; e.g., a population can be said to have a growth rate of 2 percent. The growth rate, unlike the natural increase rate, takes account of immigration and emigration. Therefore, it may differ significantly from the natural increase rate. And even in the absence of major immigration or emigration, the two rates may differ slightly because they are obtained by different methods of calculation.

General fertility rate: The total number of children born in a year per 1,000 women considered to be of childbearing age (generally 15 to 49).

Total fertility rate: Unlike the general fertility rate, which lumps all women of childbearing age together, the total fertility rate breaks down this group into five-year *cohorts*, or age brackets, and is expressed as the sum of age-specific fertility rates for all these cohorts. The total fertility rate is calculated either per woman or per 1,000 women. It takes into account not only the ages at which members of the childbearing population have children, but also the age distribution of women within this childbearing population.

Gross reproduction rate: Like the total fertility rate, it refers to age-specific birthrates for women in the childbearing years; unlike the total fertility rate, it refers to births of daughters only. It is assumed that none of the mothers will die during the span of their childbearing years.

Net reproduction rate: Calculated the same way as the gross reproduction rate, except that it takes into account death rates for each age group of mothers.

Net reproduction rate of 1: This means that a population is at replacement level.

Variants: The UN projections of future population trends consist of four variants—high, medium, low, and constant—computed according to various assumptions about the evolution of fertility.

THE WORLD IN 1970

In 1970, the population of the world was about 3.609 billion people; average life expectancy at birth was 53.9 years for men and 56.6 years for women; the total fertility rate was 4.4 per woman; 36.5 percent of the population was less than 15 years old, 58 percent between 15 and 64, and 5.5 percent over 65; 37.4 percent of the population inhabited urban areas; and there was a dependency ratio of 726.

About 70 percent of the population, or 2.5 billion people, inhabited the less developed world, and about 30 percent, or 1.1 billion people, the developed world.[1] The demographic characteristics of these two subgroups were radically different, as can be seen in Table 1. In the less developed countries, the average life expectancy was nearly 20 years lower, the total fertility rate was about 3 points higher, and there was a much higher dependency ratio.

The considerable difference in dependency ratios is perhaps the most important indicator of the heavier economic constraints that weigh on the less developed countries. The extremely high figure for these countries can be explained partly by their high proportion of young people (40.8 percent of the population under 15 years versus 26.7 percent in the developed world). It can also

---

[1]We should note that China and India together represent by themselves about half the population of the less developed world. Seven countries—China, India, the Soviet Union, the United States, Indonesia, Japan, and Brazil—accounted for 57 percent of the world's population in 1970. This figure is raised to 70 percent by the addition of eight more countries whose population exceeded 50 million: Bangladesh, Pakistan, the Federal Republic of Germany, Nigeria, the United Kingdom, Italy, France, and Mexico.

TABLE 1
World Demographic Indicators in 1970

	Total Fertility Rate*	Life Expec- tancy at Birth†	Crude Birth- rate‡	Crude Death Rate‡	Natural Increase Rate‡	Depen- dency Ratio‡	Per- cent Urban
More developed regions	2.3	71	17.2	9.2	8.0	570	66
Less developed regions	5.3	52	37.5	14.3	23.2	803	25
Total	4.4	55	31.5	12.8	18.7	726	37

*Per woman.
†Years.
‡Per thousand.
SOURCES: UN, *Population Prospects as Assessed in 1973,* pp. 20, 23, 112;
UN *World Demographic Indicators*, pp. 1–3.

be explained by a life expectancy that is clearly under 65 years, the age limit used to calculate the dependency ratio. However, in neither the developing nor the developed countries is it realistic to assume that everyone in the population age 15 to 65 actually does work, or that those outside that age group do not work. In the less developed countries, it is often the case that children start working before they are 15 years old.

Large disparities exist not only between developed and developing countries but also among the less developed countries themselves. One can distinguish countries with high birth- and death rates from those with high birthrates and low death rates. The first group, already smaller than the second and tending to diminish over time, includes much of tropical Africa and several regions in Asia and Latin America. According to Keyfitz and Flieger,[2] this demographic area includes about 500 million peo-

[2]Nathan Keyfitz and Wilhelm Flieger, *Population Facts and Methods of Demography*, W. H. Freeman & Co., San Francisco, 1971, pp. 4–6.

25

ple. The second group includes about 2 billion people, primarily in Asia and Latin America, and it is experiencing a rather notable reduction in mortality (toward a rate of 10 per thousand), although the birthrate remains high (about 40 per thousand). This situation produces a rather high rate of growth (about 3 percent annually). Obviously, this type of distinction does not take into account the differences among individual countries. However, it does constitute a useful starting point for forecasting population. Two examples will illustrate a variety of cases.[3]

Ethiopia is one of the most dramatic examples of the first type of country. Life expectancy averages 38 years (39.6 for women and 36.5 for men); the crude death rate is 25.8 per thousand. The total fertility rate is 6.7 per woman. The net reproduction rate is only 1.95, while the gross reproduction rate is 3.3; the crude birthrate is 49.4 per thousand. The growth rate is about 2.3 percent and is forecast to rise no matter what realistic hypotheses of fertility and mortality are used—one reason being that 53.3 percent of the population is less than 20 years old, a large cohort of potential parents.

Colombia is an illustration of the second type. Life expectancy averages 61 years (62.7 for women and 59.2 for men), and the death rate is very low, 8.8 per thousand. The total fertility rate and crude birthrate both remain high: 5.8 per woman and 41 per thousand. The difference between the gross reproduction rate (2.9) and the net reproduction rate (2.5) is relatively small. The overall growth rate is thus very high, 3.2 percent, but it is expected to decrease in the years to come, and, in fact, has already begun to do so.

THE EVOLUTION OF DEMOGRAPHIC INDICATORS, 1970–1990

As the figures in Table 2 show, the present gaps between the less developed and developed countries will still exist in 1990 or 1995. According to the UN medium variant, the world's 5.279 billion

[3]Data are drawn from UN, *Population Prospects as Assessed in 1973*, pp. 94, 95, 110, 111, 113, 114, 128, 129, 138, 142.

people will be divided as follows: 1.277 billion in the more developed countries and 4.001 billion in the less developed countries, respectively representing 24 and 76 percent of the total population (approximately 30 and 70 percent in 1970). The "average" person in each of these worlds will also be rather different. In the richer countries, life expectancy at birth will average 73 years; in the poorer countries, 61 years. In the richer countries there will be 540 economically inactive persons for every 1,000 members of the population; in the poorer countries, there will be 738. The total fertility rate will be about 2 points higher in the less developed countries in 1985-1990. It should be noted, however, that the demographic differences will be smaller than in 1970, with the lot of the less developed countries somewhat improved.

The death rate in developed countries will scarcely change (9.7 per thousand in 1985-1990 versus 9.2 in 1970-1975), because of the relatively large proportion of older people already in their populations. In the less developed countries, however, divergent trends will appear. For these countries as a whole, the death rate will have fallen from 14.2 per thousand in 1970-1975 to 10.4 per thousand in 1985-1990. But whereas in Africa, for example, the death rate, even with a significant decline, will remain at about 12.9 per thousand in 1990 (versus 19.8 in 1970), in Latin America it will reach the exceptionally low level of 6.2 per thousand. Those less developed countries that now have a low death rate because of their present young age structure will witness a rise in the rate caused by the aging of their populations; those that have a high death rate in spite of their young age structure will see the rate decrease because of improved health and other socioeconomic conditions; this will be a clearer trend than the increase in the death rate.

The population of the developed countries is expected to increase because of the absolute numbers of people in their childbearing years, even though fertility rates are likely to fall; according to the UN projections the birthrate in these countries will stablize at 17 per thousand in 1985-1990 (as opposed to 17.2 per thousand in 1970-1975), and according to the low variant, fertility will have declined to below replacement level in

TABLE 2
World Demographic Indicators in 1990

	TFR*† (per woman)		E (yr)		CBR (per 1,000)		CDR (per 1,000)		NIR (per 1,000)		DR	Pop 20y (%)	Pop Urb (%)	Total Population (in 1,000s)
More developed regions														
C*	...	...	72.6	73.0	17.6	17.0	9.7	9.7	...	...	...	...	...	1,297,363
M	2.2	2.2	72.6	73.0	16.8	16.0	9.8	9.9	7.0	6.1	539.7	31.1	77.0	1,277,570
H	2.5	2.5	72.6	73.0	18.6	17.8	9.6	9.6	9.0	8.2	579.0	33.0	78.7	1,313,966
L	2.0	2.0	72.6	73.0	15.3	14.5	9.9	10.1	5.4	4.4	508.8	29.5	75.3	1,249,919
Less developed regions														
C	...	...	59.4	61.4	38.8	38.5	10.5	9.5	...	...	...	...	...	4,280,818
M	4.3	4.0	58.7	60.7	32.3	30.2	10.4	9.4	21.9	20.7	737.6	48.5	35.0	4,001,471
H	4.7	4.4	59.4	67.5	34.7	32.8	10.2	9.2	24.5	23.6	783.1	50.0	37.1	4,128,107
L	4.0	3.5	57.0	58.8	30.5	27.7	11.2	10.2	19.4	17.5	686.4	46.7	33.1	3,837,943

World total

C	...	...	61.1	62.7	33.7	33.7	10.3	9.5	9.5	...	...	...	...	5,578,181
M	3.8	3.5	60.7	62.4	28.4	26.8	10.2	9.5	18.2	17.3	685.2	44.3	45.2	5,279,041
H	4.2	4.0	61.4	63.1	30.7	29.3	10.1	9.3	20.6	20.0	729.1	45.9	67.1	5,444,073
L	3.5	3.2	59.2	60.8	26.7	24.6	10.8	10.2	15.8	14.4	639.0	42.5	43.5	5,087,863

Abbreviations: TFR, total fertility rate; E, life expectancy; CBR, crude birthrate; CDR, crude death rate; NIR, natural increase rate; DR, dependency ratio; Pop 20 y, proportion of people under 20 in total population; Pop Urb, proportion of urban residents in total population. Variants: C, constant; M, medium; H, high; L, low.

†Where there are two vertical columns under one heading, the periods 1985–1990 and 1990–1995 are used.

SOURCE: UN, *Population Prospects as Assessed in 1973*, pp. 20, 23, 113; UN, *Selected World Demographic Indicators*, pp. 1–3.

1980–1985. This evolution, however, will probably not be smooth, since short-term changes in births and deaths may cause fluctuations. The long-term decrease in fertility will produce a slight aging of the population (according to the medium variant, the proportion of those over 65 will increase from 9.6 percent in 1970 to 11.3 percent in 1990). Or this aging will be brought about by a reduction in mortality if mortality is greater among older people than among youth. However, it is more likely that the reduction in mortality will be greater among the young, that their age cohorts will thus be enlarged, and that this will contribute to a reduction, rather than an increase, in the average age of the population.

The dependency ratio in the developed countries will also improve by 1990, since it is more strongly influenced by a reduction in fertility than by an increase in life expectancy. Depending upon which variant is used—509 (low) or 540 (medium), the improvement will vary notably; in either case it will be a contrast to the 1970 figure of 570. As in the case of fertility, the evolution of the dependency ratio will not be smooth, but fluctuations should be small.

In the less developed countries, the rate of decrease in the birthrate will depend on which fertility variant is used in the calculations. Beginning with a birthrate of 36.6 to 38.1 per thousand in 1970–1975, the range of possibilities in 1985–1990 extends from 34.7, based upon the high variant, to 30.5, using the low variant.

According to the UN high-variant projections, the growth rate for the entire world will average about 2 percent annually—a very high rate—through the 1980s. In the best case, according to the low variant, this growth rate will decline to approximately 1.6 percent in 1985–1990 (1.9 percent for the less developed countries alone). Assuming a 2 percent world growth rate, total world population will reach 5.279 billion in 1990. Thirty-five percent of that number will be less than 15 years old, 59 percent between 15 and 64 years old, and 6 percent above 65 years. Life expectancies at birth will average 70 years for men and 64 years for women. The dependency ratio will be 685 per thousand.

However, no one should be terribly concerned at this level of aggregation. More striking are the differences between regions and groups, some of which have already been indicated. In addition, as Table 3 shows, the population distribution by continent is going to change. And within the less developed world there will be further disparities. In South Asia and Latin America, the rates of growth will increase through 1975–1980 and then begin to decline; in Africa, they will remain high throughout the period (see Table 4). Africa will see its population increase from 352 million to 614 million, Latin America from 283 to 486 million, and South Asia from 1.1 billion to 1.836 billion. A much more detailed breakdown of changes throughout the world is given in the Appendix at the end of the volume, which presents the UN calculations of likely population increases and percentage growth rates for 242 countries in five-year periods from 1970 to 2000.

TABLE 3
Geographic Distribution of World Population, by Large Regions,
in 1970 and in 1990 (Percent)

	1970	1990
Developed areas	30	24
Less developed areas	70	76
World Total	100	100
Africa	9.7	11.6
Latin America	7.8	9.2
North America	6.2	5.2
East Asia	25.5	23.3
South Asia	30.6	24.8
Europe	12.6	9.7
Oceania	0.5	0.5
U.S.S.R.	6.7	5.6

SOURCE: UN, *World Demographic Indicators*, pp. 90–97.

TABLE 4
Evolution of Growth Rates in South Asia, Latin America, and Africa (Percent), Medium Variant

	1970–1975	1975–1980	1980–1985	1985–1990
South Asia	2.53	2.65	2.60	2.45
Latin America	2.71	2.74	2.71	2.64
Africa	2.64	2.77	2.86	2.88

SOURCE: UN, *Population Prospects as Assessed in 1973*, p. 16.

THE WORLD IN 1990—DERIVATIVE PROJECTIONS: URBANIZATION AND THE LABOR FORCE

Projections of the distribution of population between rural and urban areas are derived from global population projections, and the definition of rural and urban areas is based on each country's definitions as noted in the *Demographic Yearbook* of the UN. For countries about which information is not available, estimates are generally made by comparison with similar countries. Sometimes, most notably in the case of China, they are based on special studies. The UN has used three hypotheses about the evolution of the rate of urbanization which, combined with the three hypotheses (high, medium, and low) of population growth rates, yield nine series of projections. The results presented here are limited principally to the most probable, "medium-medium" variants (medium variant for the total population linked to medium variant for the rate of urbanization).[4]

---

[4]An urbanization hypothesis is constructed as follows. The difference in population increase rates between the urban and rural populations observed in the period 1950–1970 is averaged for 1960 to define the initial level; the average urban-rural growth difference in 1960 for the entire world, 2.75 percent, thus provides the base for projections of the final level that will be reached by all countries in the year 2000. It is assumed that each country will reach the final level in a linear path even though, in reality, short-range drops and rises may

32

What are the results of the UN projections? In 1990, about 45 percent of the population of the world will live in urban areas, versus less than 38 percent in 1970. That proportion will increase for the developed world from 66 to 77 percent, and for the less developed world from 25 to 35 percent. (Since the UN uses a single model for all countries and regions of the world, more refined geographical differences cannot be assessed.) Projections of urbanization are used to develop projections of the growth of metropolitan areas. (See Table 5 for the projected growth of the world's 50 largest metropolitan regions from 1950 to 2000.)

What are the implications of increasing urbanization? Generally speaking it is associated with certain types of problems. But comparative rates of urbanization do not denote much when one studies countries at radically different levels of development. Clearly, the inhabitants of Cairo will not live in the same way as those of the Egyptian countryside, and Egyptain public officials will not confront the same problems in the one case as in the other. Nevertheless, there are few basic comparisons that can be made between Cairo and, say, Chicago. For any given country, the evolution of the urbanization rate has its own specific meaning. In Egypt, for example, the projected change in the proportion of urban residents from 44 percent in 1970 to 58 percent in 1990 directly reflects changes in certain national demographic indicators. A comparison between two countries—even *within* the less developed or the developed world—has meaning only when it involves homogenous regional areas.

Projections for the labor force, like those for urbanization, are derived from UN figures—in this case, those of the International Labor Organization (ILO). The size of the labor force is assumed to be related to the population's rate of growth, to its age structure, and to age-specific work-participation rates. By 1990, the growth rate will have had hardly any effect on the age structure

---

occur. Mathematically extrapolating the 1960 levels to the year 2000 gives the final result, from which the rate of urbanization can be calculated. This method is perfectly arbitrary and is not based on any particular behavioral theory of urbanization. No relationship is assumed between the fertility rate and the urbanization rate.

TABLE 5

World's 50 Largest Agglomerations, Ranked by Size and Population in Millions, 1960–2000

Rank	1960		1970		1975		1980		1990		2000	
1.	New York–N.E. N.J.	14.2	New York–N.E. N.J.	16.3	Tokyo–Yokohama	17.3	Tokyo–Yokohama	19.7	Tokyo–Yokohama	23.5	Mexico City	31.6
2.	London	10.8	Tokyo–Yokohama	14.9	New York–N.E. N.J.	17.0	New York–N.E. N.J.	17.9	Mexico City	21.6	Tokyo–Yokohama	26.1
3.	Tokyo–Yokohama	10.7	London	10.5	Mexico City	10.9	Mexico City	13.9	New York–N.E. N.J.	20.1	São Paulo	26.0
4.	Rhine–Ruhr	8.7	Shanghai	10.0	Shanghai	10.9	São Paulo	12.5	São Paulo	18.7	New York–N.E. N.J.	22.2
5.	Shanghai	7.4	Rhine–Ruhr	9.3	London	10.7	Shanghai	12.0	Shanghai	14.9	Calcutta	19.7
6.	Paris	7.4	Mexico City	8.6	São Paulo	10.0	London	11.0	Seoul	14.3	Rio de Janeiro	19.4
7.	Buenos Aires	6.7	Paris	8.4	Rhine–Ruhr	9.7	Los Angeles–Long Beach	10.7	Peking	14.2	Shanghai	19.2
8.	Los Angeles–Long Beach	6.5	Los Angeles–Long Beach	8.4	Los Angeles–Long Beach	9.5	Buenos Aires	10.4	Rio de Janeiro	14.1	Greater Bombay	19.1
9.	Moscow	6.3	Buenos Aires	8.3	Buenos Aires	9.3	Peking	10.2	Calcutta	13.7	Peking	19.1
10.	Chicago–N.W. Indiana	6.0	São Paulo	7.8	Paris	9.2	Rio de Janeiro	10.0	Greater Bombay	13.1	Seoul	18.7
11.	Osaka–Kobe	5.7	Osaka–Kobe	7.6	Osaka–Kobe	8.7	Rhine–Ruhr	9.9	Los Angeles–Long Beach	13.0	Jakarta	16.9

Rank	City					
12.	Calcutta	Moscow 5.5	Peking 7.1	Peking 8.5	Paris 9.9	Buenos Aires 12.3 / Cairo–Giza–Imbaba 16.4
13.	**Mexico City**	Peking 4.9	Rio de Janeiro 7.0	Rio de Janeiro 8.3	Osaka–Kobe 9.7	Cairo–Giza–Imbaba 12.0 / Karachi 15.9
14.	Milan	Calcutta 4.5	Calcutta 6.9	Calcutta 8.1	Calcutta 9.6	London 11.7 / Los Angeles–Long Beach 14.8
15.	Peking	Rio de Janeiro 4.5	Moscow 6.9	Moscow 7.6	Seoul 9.4	Jakarta 11.5 / Buenos Aires 14.0
16.	Rio de Janeiro	Chicago–N.W. Indiana 4.4	Seoul 6.7	Seoul 7.3	Greater Bombay 8.7	Osaka–Kobe 11.4 / Teheran 13.8
17.	São Paulo	Greater Bombay 4.4	Greater Bombay 5.8	Greater Bombay 7.1	Cairo–Giza–Imbaba 8.4	**Paris** 11.2 / Delhi 13.2
18.	Greater Bombay	Cairo–Giza–Imbaba 4.1	Chicago–N.W. Indiana 5.7	Chicago–N.W. Indiana 7.1	Moscow 8.2	Rhine–Ruhr 10.6 / London 12.7
19.	Cairo–Giza–Imbaba	Milan 3.7	Cairo–Giza–Imbaba 5.5	Cairo–Giza–Imbaba 6.9	Chicago–N.W. Indiana 7.5	Karachi 10.2 / Manila 12.7
20.	Philadelphia–N.J.	Seoul 3.6	Milan 5.4	Milan 6.0	Jakarta 7.2	Teheran 9.4 / Osaka–Kobe 12.6
21.	Detroit	Jakarta 3.5	Jakarta 4.3	Jakarta 5.6	Milan 6.5	Moscow 9.4 / **Paris** 12.3
22.	Leningrad	Philadelphia–N.J. 3.5	Delhi 4.0	Delhi 4.5	Karachi 6.0	Delhi 9.0 / Lima–Callao 12.1
23.	Tientsin	Tientsin 3.4	Karachi 4.0	Karachi 4.5	Teheran 5.8	Manila 8.6 / Rhine–Ruhr 11.3
24.	Naples	Detroit 3.2	Manila 4.0	Manila 4.4	Delhi 5.7	Chicago–N.W. Indiana 8.4 / Bangkok–Thonburi 11.0

TABLE 5 (Continued)
World's 50 Largest Agglomerations, Ranked by Size and Population in Millions, 1960–2000

Rank	1960		1970		1975		1980		1990		2000	
25.	Hong Kong	2.7	Leningrad	4.0	Teheran	4.4	Manila	5.6	Lima–Callao	8.3	Baghdad	10.9
26.	Jakarta	2.7	Hong Kong	3.7	Tientsin	4.3	Lima–Callao	5.2	Baghdad	7.5	Moscow	10.6
27.	Birmingham	2.7	Naples	3.6	Leningrad	4.3	Tientsin	4.7	Milan	7.4	Madras	10.4
28.	Manchester	2.5	Delhi	3.5	Philadel-phia–N.J.	4.2	Madras	4.7	Madras	7.1	Bogota	9.5
29.	Shenyang	2.5	Manila	3.5	Detroit	4.2	Leningrad	4.6	Bangkok–Thonburi	7.0	Lagos	9.4
30.	San Fran-cisco–Oakland	2.4	Teheran	3.4	Hong Kong	4.0	Baghdad	4.6	Bogota	6.8	Chicago–N.W. Indiana	9.3
31.	Katowice	2.4	Karachi	3.3	Lima–Callao	3.9	Detroit	4.5	Istanbul	6.0	Kinshasa	9.1
32.	Boston	2.4	Madrid	3.1	Naples	3.8	Philadel-phia–N.J.	4.5	Tientsin	5.8	Istanbul	8.3
33.	Seoul	2.4	Madras	3.0	Madras	3.7	Bogota	4.4	Kinshasa	5.6	Milan	8.3
34.	Delhi	2.3	San Fran-cisco–Oakland	3.0	Madrid	3.6	Hong Kong	4.3	Lagos	5.4	Lahore	7.7
35.	Madrid	2.3	Rome	2.9	Baghdad	3.4	Bangkok–Thonburi	4.3	Leningrad	5.3	Tientsin	7.5
36.	Rome	2.3	Lima–Callao	2.9	Bogota	3.4	Madrid	4.1	Detroit	5.1	Rangoon	7.4
37.	Manila	2.2	Shenyang	2.8	Bangkok–Thonburi	3.3	Naples	4.0	Philadel-phia–N.J.	5.1	Guadalajara	6.2

No.												
38.	Wuhan	2.2	Birmingham	2.8	Istanbul	3.3	Istanbul	4.0	Lahore	5.1	Lyallpur	6.2
39.	Berlin	2.2	Katowice	2.8	Rome	3.2	Rome	3.5	Madrid	5.0	Leningrad	6.1
40.	Chungking	2.2	Montreal	2.7	San Francisco–Oakland	3.2	Santiago	3.5	Hong Kong	5.0	Caracas	6.0
41.	Sydney	2.1	Santiago	2.7	Santiago	3.1	San Francisco–Oakland	3.4	Rangoon	4.9	Dacca	5.9
42.	Hamburg	2.1	Sydney	2.7	Montreal	3.0	Montreal	3.4	Caracas	4.6	Madrid	5.9
43.	Montreal	2.0	Boston	2.6	Wuhan	3.0	Wuhan	3.4	Naples	4.5	Wuhan	5.8
44.	Kwangchow (Canton)	2.0	Istanbul	2.6	Sydney	3.0	Sydney	3.3	Wuhan	4.4	Belo Horizonte	5.7
45.	Glasgow	1.9	Bogota	2.6	Katowice	2.9	Katowice	3.3	Santiago	4.3	Detroit	5.7
46.	Leeds–Bradford	1.9	Wuhan	2.6	Birmingham	2.9	Caracas	3.2	Guadalajara	4.2	Philadelphia–N.J.	5.6
47.	Santiago	1.9	Toronto	2.5	Shenyang	2.9	Toronto	3.2	Montreal	4.2	Alexandria	5.6
48.	Teheran	1.9	Baghdad	2.5	Toronto	2.9	Lahore	3.1	Alexandria	4.1	Hong Kong	5.5
49.	Karachi	1.8	Manchester	2.5	Washington, D.C.–Md.–Va.	2.8	Rangoon	3.1	Rome	4.1	Ahmedabad	5.5
50.	Melbourne	1.8	Bangkok–Thonburi	2.5	Athens	2.8	Washington, D.C.–Md.–Va.	3.1	Belo Horizonte	4.0	Bangalore	5.4

SOURCE: UN, Department of Economic and Social Affairs, Population Division, "*Trends and Prospects in the Population of Urban Agglomerations, 1950–2000, as Assessed in 1973–1975*," working paper no. 58 (New York, Nov. 21, 1975), p. 61.

of the labor force; for all practical purposes, all the future members of the labor force of 1990 were already born in 1970–1975. The only factor that might have a significant effect on the labor force is the work-participation rate. There will not be major changes in this rate for the already heavily employed male population; but for women, behavioral changes in the next decade may have a significant impact. As the status and education levels of women rise they will probably have fewer children, and this will be one reason why more of them will work.

The ILO uses the following hypotheses (which do not take into account international migration): that male participation rates at all ages will decrease in both developed and less developed countries, that female participation rates will increase in the developed countries for ages 20 to 64 and will decrease for ages under 20 and over 64, and that female participation rates will decrease for all ages in the underdeveloped countries.[5] While the hypotheses on the developed countries seem to be realistic, those for the less developed countries—in particular, the reduction in the female participation rate—do not. According to a supplementary study of work-force projections carried out by the ILO, female participation rates always tend to fall as a country begins the process of economic development, because of the large reduction in the numbers of people working in agriculture, a large percentage of which are women.[6] However, this general assumption of the ILO is somewhat misleading, since only a small number of populous less developed countries like India and Indonesia account for this trend, whereas there are divergent trends in certain countries and regional groupings that are less populated (for example, the Arab countries). In any case, the term *participation in the labor force* is rather imprecise in economies where wage earners constitute a small part of the population.

[5]According to several documents presented at the Bucharest World Population Conference in 1974 and other complementary studies. These projections were calculated on the basis of the 1968 UN projections. New projections based on 1973 are currently being carried out.

[6]See ILO, *World and Regional Labor Force Prospects to the Year 2000*, paper for World Population Conference, Bucharest, 1974 (E/CONF60/CBP/31).

THE LARGE REGIONAL AREAS

The dichotomy between developed and less developed countries reflects basic demographic differences between the two areas, each taken as a whole. However, it is useful to refine the analysis of the less developed world by considering some of its large geographic and cultural groupings. The following survey is limited to four groups: Latin America, the Indian subcontinent, the Middle East, and China.

Latin America

In 1970 Latin America (South America, Central America, and the Caribbean) had 283 million inhabitants, 7.8 percent of the world's population. This region had experienced the highest rate of growth in the world during the previous 20 years (on the order of 2.8 percent per year), which if sustained would produce a doubling of the population in 25 years. This is the result of considerable progress made in increasing life expectancy, which went from 52.3 years in 1950–1955 to 61.4 years in 1970–1975, while fertility remained high (the total fertility rate was 5.6 per woman in 1970–1975, with no significant decreases for the last decade except in a very limited number of countries, principally Argentina, Uruguay, Cuba, and Chile). These trends are reflected in crude birth- and death rates of, respectively, 41 and 14 per thousand in 1950–1955 versus 37 and 9 per thousand in 1970–1975. The consequence is a very young age structure (52 percent less than 20 years old and only 4 percent over 65) and a very high dependency ratio. Population density is low throughout Latin America (the average was 16 inhabitants per square kilometer in 1970), but there are rather significant differences among regions. The Caribbean averages 103 inhabitants per square kilometer, with certain small areas having very high densities (Barbados, 555; Martinique, 307; Puerto Rico, 308); Central America averages 27 inhabitants per square kilometer, with 26 in Mexico; and South America averages 10 inhabitants per square kilometer in the Temperate Zone and 11 in the Tropical Zone, which corresponds more or less to the densities in Argentina, 9, and Brazil, 11. However, figures for average density do not truly indicate the

39

population distribution, since 57 percent, a rather high proportion, lives in urban areas.

Despite local variations, Latin American countries can be roughly divided into three categories: those that still have high mortality and fertility rates, those—the large majority—that have already made great progress in life expectancy but maintain high fertility rates, and those that have reached mortality and fertility approaching the levels of the developed countries. Bolivia (life expectancy of 46.8 years and total fertility rate of 6.1 per woman) is typical of the first group; Brazil (life expectancy of 61.4 years and total fertility rate of 5) is in the second category; and Argentina (life expectancy of 68.2 years and total fertility rate of 3) is in the third. The countries that are most highly urbanized have generally been the most successful in controlling both fertility and mortality: the urban population is 35 percent in Bolivia, 55 percent in Brazil, and 77 percent in Argentina. Nevertheless, this is not a cause-and-effect relationship; historical factors and specific national characteristics play an important role.

The current situation in Latin America presents a rather high potential for growth, partly because of the rising life expectancy already mentioned, which should improve still further—to 67.3 years in 1985–1990, reaching 68.8 years in 1990–1995—and partly because of the current very high level of fertility, the most important factor, which will remain high even though it will decline throughout the coming decades whatever calculations are used (see Table 6). The young age structure will only reinforce this trend. Nevertheless, the growth rate, rather high in any case, will vary depending on the calculations used. According to the high variant, it will continue to increase through 1990; according to the low variant, it will be reduced in the near future; and according to the medium variant, it will decline after 1985.

High fertility rates notwithstanding, an improvement in the dependency ratio is forecast: from the 1970 figure of 867 per thousand to 852, 793, or 730 per thousand in 1990, depending, respectively, on the use of high, medium, or low variants. If the low variant is realized, the reduction will be particularly marked.

Like fertility and growth rates, urbanization rates in Latin America will continue to be high; the urban population is expected to reach 68 percent by 1990.

TABLE 6
Total Fertility Rate in Latin America

	Variant	1970–1975	1985–1990	1990–1995
	Medium	5.3	4.5	4.2
Total fertility rate (per woman)	High	5.3	5.0	4.9
	Low	5.2	3.9	3.5

SOURCE: UN, *World Demographic Indicators*, p. 60.

Throughout the region, the demographic distribution will change. The countries in the South Temperate Zone (Argentina, Uruguay, and Chile), which constituted 12.7 percent of the population of the region in 1970 and in which the decline in fertility over the past decade has been greatest, will not represent more than 10 percent of the total by 1990. Most striking is the projection that the population of Argentina, 25 percent of Brazil's population in 1970, will be no more than 18 percent of Brazil's in 1990.

The Indian Subcontinent

That part of Asia south of the Himalayas—essentially India, Sri Lanka, Bangladesh, and Pakistan—had about 700 million inhabitants in 1970. Here, more than elsewhere, projections of the future are extremely pessimistic because of the size of the populations involved, their tremendous socioeconomic problems, the lack of real progress in recent years in limiting population growth and improving economic standards, and the limited availability of natural resources.

At the present the major demographic indicators are as follows. Life expectancy in 1970–1975 was on the order of 50 to 55 years, a noteworthy improvement over the previous two decades, largely attributable to progress in reducing infant mortality. Yet infant mortality levels still remain rather high. With the exception of Sri Lanka, whose infant mortality rate is no more than 50 per thousand, the rate is nowhere lower than 100 per thousand—in most cases about 150 per thousand and in some cases (Nepal) as high as 200 per thousand. One particularly important characteristic of the region is that the life expectancy of men is higher than that of women (most notably in Bangladesh and Pakistan). This gap is generally attributed to the significance of deaths in childbirth, but there are other reasons, too, since the higher female mortality rates include groups not of childbearing age.[7]

The figures for population density, although much higher than the world average, give only an approximate idea of the extreme concentration of population in certain rural areas of this region and the pressure this exerts on food resources. On the one hand, large parts of the territories involved are deserts or high mountains, and on the other hand, industrialization and urbanization rates are low (in 1975 the proportion of urbanized inhabitants was 24 percent in Pakistan, 20 percent in India, and 6 percent in Bangladesh). Bangladesh illustrates in a startling way the dramatic character of the situation and its ineluctable evolution. In 1970, the density of the essentially rural population was 474 inhabitants per square kilometer; by 1990 it is expected to reach 750 according to the low variant and 850 according to the high variant.

Whatever variant is used, the population of the Indian subcontinent is going to undergo considerable growth, and its present socioeconomic difficulties are bound to increase, especially in three areas:

1. The problem of the large urban areas, which include several hundred thousand if not several million people, is certain to get worse, primarily in India and Pakistan. In the Indian census of 1970, Calcutta had 7.01 million inhabitants, Bombay 5.7 million, Delhi 3.6 million, and Madras 3.2 million. In the Pakistani census of 1972, Karachi had 3.5 million. In both countries urbanization is not an indicator of industrialization but rather a reflection of the demographic-economic disequilibria of the countryside. The attraction of the cities creates a supplementary problem without really relieving pressures in rural areas.

[7]J. C. Chesnais and J. Vallin, "Les Populations au Sud de l'Himalaya," *Population*, no. 6, Paris, November–December 1975, pp. 1059–1110.

2. Demographic pressures on agricultural resources are such that it would be a delusion to hope that improvements in agricultural techniques will offset them, as in Boserup's scheme.[8] Efforts to improve living conditions will come up against a double geographic and financial limitation mechanism that can be outlined as follows:

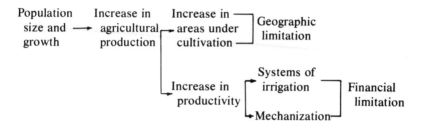

3. The gravity of the present situation and hence the multiplicity of high-priority objectives, which are impossible to satisfy simultaneously with the limited financial means available (in particular the low accumulation of capital), may be the cause of conflicts and serious tensions. For example, an effort to increase educational opportunities ought to involve expanded popular acceptance of contraceptive practices, but what happens if this cuts the funding for an irrigation program? Similarly, while expanded education might reduce fertility, it could also increase the rural exodus and urban unemployment. The determination of an optimal population-control strategy necessarily implies sacrifices for people who may already have reached their limits of toleration.

Although the present and future situations are not as bleak in India as elsewhere (especially in Bangladesh), India's giant population (second in the world) and the lessons that can be learned from its efforts in family planning make it the most important example.

---

[8]Esther Boserup, *The Conditions of Agricultural Growth: The Economics of Agrarian Change under Population Pressure*, George Allen & Unwin, London, 1975.

In the census of April 1, 1971, India had 548 million inhabitants. A half-dozen projections were made from the census data, each one consisting of several fertility and mortality hypotheses. Although there was reasonably solid agreement about the figures from which the hypotheses were drawn, the various calculations made from these figures produced results that are quite different. For 1986–1991, for example, figures for life expectancy range from 51 to 67 years for women and from 53 to 68 years for men. If one uses the life expectancy figure of 50 years in 1970 and that medium hypothesis according to which life expectancy should increase about six months annually from now to the end of the century—the life expectancy rates for women progressing slightly faster than those of men, so that by 1991 the current gap between female and male life expectancies will be narrowed—it will take until 1990 for life expectancy to reach 60 years. The differences in fertility projections are even more striking, starting from the base calculations of a total fertility rate of about 6 per woman and a birthrate of 42 per thousand. The authors of the various projections all agree that the modest but certain decline in fertility of the last decade is going to continue, but at what rate remains uncertain. The six projections foresee for 1991 populations varying from 730 million to 900 million. Medium variants range from 801 million to 876 million, as can be seen in Table 7.

An analysis of the nature and effectiveness of Indian policy for regulating demographic growth permits us to estimate how optimistic or pessimistic are the hypotheses used in making the projections. Moreover, because India was one of the first countries to implement a population-control policy, a study of the stages of this policy as well as its successes and failures provides important lessons for other countries.

Ignoring the minimal first efforts, which date back to the 1920s, one can trace the beginning of the Indian policy of demographic control to the early 1950s. This policy was implemented in several phases. During the first phase, that of the "clinical approach," it was thought that a medical infrastructure had to be developed, and this led to efforts to increase the number of clinics and to train medical students and paramedical professionals in the techniques of family planning. Judging by the results of the census

TABLE 7
India: Estimates of Total Population (in Millions), Medium Variants

	1971	1981	1991
Raghavachari	547	668	801
Ambannavar	548	683	839
ORG	585	719	859
	585	707	822
Registrar General	547	668	801
Cassen and Dyson	557	688	829
	557	681	808
UN	543	694	876

SOURCES: Other than the projections made by the UN and national statistical services, see Committee for International Coordination of National Research and Demography, (CICRED), *The Population of India*, Paris, 1974; "Population Projections 1976–2001," in *Population in India's Development 1947–2000*, Ashish Bose et al. (eds.), Vikas Publishing House, New Delhi, 1974; J. P. Ambannavar, *Population*, The Macmillan Co. of India, New Delhi, 1975; Operations Research Group (ORG), "Population of India—A Projection, 1971–2001," mimeo., Baroda, India, undated; R. Cassen and T. Dyson, "New Projections for India," *Population and Development Review*, vol. 2, no. 1, March 1976, pp. 101–136.

of 1961, the efforts seem to have been largely in vain. The growth rate was higher than had been foreseen.

The clinical approach . . . reached only a relatively small fraction of the people . . . [and] gave way to the "extension approach" in which an extensive campaign was launched through mass media, individual contacts, and community group efforts to motivate persons to adopt family planning and the small family norm. Since attitudes on family planning are greatly influenced by social leaders, a large number of orientation camps for educating the village leaders . . . were held.[9]

[9]Committee for International Coordination of National Research in Demography (CICRED), *The Population of India*, Paris, 1974, p. 144.

These efforts were guided by a quantitative objective established in the Third Demographic Plan: the reduction of the birthrate to 25 per thousand by 1973. Among the techniques recommended were the intrauterine device (IUD) and the cervical cap (CC), although sterilization was emphasized and has been even more widely promoted in recent years. But in spite of a reduction in fertility after 1965–1966, the expected goal was not attained, and a subsequent demographic plan set the target birthrate at 30 per thousand by 1979.

In reviewing the limited results of family planning in India before the more recent and harsher methods were employed (some attempts were made to forcibly round men up for sterilization), one should remember that during the first years of the family-planning program there was no country with comparable experience upon which the public authorities could base their choice of methods, Indian society was more than 80 percent rural and distributed in an enormous number of villages, the level of literacy and the social status of women both lagged, and the population was hardly prepared for a change in behavior. Thus, the family-planning program had to create a new state of mind and sensitize the population to the problems of demographic growth, tasks that could not be achieved overnight.

In addition, the early family-planning techniques used had almost no effect on one significant factor: the marital age. Although the marital age has been raised during the last few decades, this has been a consequence of urbanization and the expansion of the educational system, and it still is rather low in both urban and rural areas. Up to 1930 the median age of marriage was 18.6 years for men and 12.7 years for women, and it scarcely varied. A law passed in April 1930 prohibited the marriage of females younger than 14 and males younger than 18. The median age rose continuously thereafter, and by 1971, according to provisional figures, reached 22.7 years for men and 17.2 years for women, an increase of about four years. This increase might lead one to conclude that public policies could have an appreciable effect in changing the marital age. In any case, such a change is a long-term objective that implies radical modifications in behavior profoundly affecting Indian culture.

The Middle East

The demographic situation of the countries of the Middle East—the Persian Gulf states, Syria, Egypt, Lebanon, and Jordan, but excluding Cyprus, Israel, and Turkey—is so poorly known to us that it would be very risky to make an analysis based on the limited available data. The last census in Lebanon was taken in 1932; for most of the countries concerned, there are no census results at all, either because no census has ever been taken or because census results are not yet available. Registration of births and deaths is often nonexistent. Thus, the estimates of the population of Oman vary from 450,000 to 667,000 (the UN figure) to 1.5 million (the official figure). The population of the entire region was about 71 million in 1970, a quantity whose rate of growth will have almost no effect on the overall evolution of the world population. However, the considerable role that certain Middle Eastern countries play in the production and export of oil makes their demographic situation somewhat special. Their low population densities are one reason for the lack of industrial infrastructures that use up large amounts of capital; thus large proportions of their oil revenues, which they cannot absorb at home, are being invested abroad.

Several facts, however, can be extrapolated from what disparate population information is available. Mortality rates are very high; infant mortality rates are in certain cases higher than 100 per thousand, and with overall mortality rates on the order of 15 per thousand, the annual population growth rate must be around 3 percent. About 55 percent of the population is less than 20 years old, and scarcely 3 percent is more than 65 years old. Efforts are being made to reduce infant mortality and illiteracy, but it is difficult to see what the immediate or future effect of these efforts will be.

Taking into account the low life expectancy at the beginning of the period 1970–1990 and a very high fertility rate that will probably remain high or even increase during this period, one can question the plausibility of projected gains in life expectancy and still expect a substantial increase in population, which should reach 124 million by 1990 according to the UN medium

47

variant. The growth in population will increase the capacity of the oil-producing countries to absorb their income, assuming some modification in the distribution of income within these countries.

Another factor meriting attention is the high level and diverse patterns of internal and external migration that characterize the region: refugees, nomad groups, "brain drain," and most important, migration of workers toward the oil-producing states. The unequal distribution of resources among the countries involved and the diversity in their economic growth rates and educational systems suggest that there will continue to be significant migratory movements in the years to come. Saudi Arabia and Kuwait will be the principal countries for immigration. In Saudi Arabia the demand for skilled and semiskilled labor exceeds supply, although there is actually a surplus of nonskilled labor. This shortage will be met by importation of workers from other countries. A similar immigration pattern is probable in Kuwait, although the proportion of foreigners (mostly Jordanians and Palestinians) in its total population is already very high— about 53 percent—and is bound to decrease as indigenous population growth exceeds immigration.[10]

China

With respect to China, the first question still remains, what is the total population? The only census taken in China dates back to 1953. Since then, the Chinese have given certain indications about the total size of the population and the birth- and mortality rates for the period 1953 to 1957. But since 1958 no official figures have been published. In 1964 it seems that some sort of population count took place,[11] but it is not clear whether this was a national census or a more limited survey.

[10]J. A. Socknet, "Labor Market Conditions and Prospects in the Gulf States and Saudi Arabia," June 1975, p. 6. (Mimeographed.)

[11]See, for instance, P. Paillat and A. Sauvy, "La Population de la Chine, Évolution and Perspectives," *Population*, no. 3, May–June 1974, pp. 535–552.

What data do we have?[12] The census of 1953 lists the population of mainland China at 583 million persons.[13] For the same year, according to the Director of the Census, the birthrate was 37 per thousand, the death rate 17 per thousand, and the growth rate 2 percent. In 1957, the last year for which information is available, the birth- and death rates fell, respectively, to 34 and 11 per thousand. The Chinese have also given the following rates of growth for the population: 2 percent for the years 1949–1953 and 2.4 percent for 1953–1957. That is virtually all we have from official sources.

In the sixties, based on sparse information compiled from Chinese journals and radio broadcasts over the previous few years, it was thought that China had a total population of slightly over 700 million persons.[14] The problem is that it is not known whether these bits of information derive from the results of the supposed enumeration of 1964 or are more recent figures (from 1967–1968). If the former is true, then the growth rate between 1957 and 1965 has to have been between 1.32 and 1.50 percent. If the latter is true, the growth rate must have been even lower.

[12]See Leo A. Orleans, "A Selective Bibliography of the Demography of China," *Population Index*, vol. 42, no. 4, October 1976, pp. 653–693. In this paragraph, we have made use of three main calculations of China's actual and projected population: UN, *World Demographic Indicators*, p. 99; John S. Aird, *Population Policy and Demographic Prospects in the People's Republic of China: An Economic Assessment*, report to the U.S. Congress, Senate, Joint Economic Committee, 92nd Cong., 2nd sess., 1972, U.S. Government Printing Office, Washington, D.C., pp. 220–331; and L. Orleans, "China's Population Figures: Can the Contradictions Be Resolved?" *Studies in Family Planning*, vol. 7, no. 2, February 1976, pp. 52–57. See also K. C. Yeh and Carolyn Lee, "Communist China's Population Problem in the 1980s," Rand Paper P-5143, Rand Corp., Santa Monica, Calif. 1973, also published in *Issues and Studies* (Taipei), vol. 10, no. 6, March 1974, pp. 14–29.

[13]See Chen Ta, "New China's Population Census of 1953 and Its Relations to National Reconstruction and Demographic Research," *Review of the International Statistical Institute* (Stockholm), vol. 36, no. 2, 1956, pp. 255–271. If Taiwan and the overseas Chinese are included, the figure comes to 602 million, as listed in the official results of the census.

[14]Yet the *People's Daily* (Peking) spoke at that time of "more than 800 million today."

A comparison of the different official figures that are available brings out the following contradiction: If one begins with the data for 1953 and takes into account the birth- and death rates that are known (up to 1957) or estimated (since 1958), the derived population figures for 1974 do not correspond to the figures given by the Chinese at international conferences; that is, the current population is larger than admitted, the birthrate is much lower than had been believed, or the census of 1953 overestimated the size of the population. The last hypothesis must be put to one side.[15]

If the birth- and death rates given by the Chinese in 1957 are accepted and if a growth rate of 2 percent since 1957 is assumed, China's population would have surpassed 900 million in 1974. As Table 8 shows, for 1970 the UN gives the figures of 772 million, L. Orleans proposes 738 million, and John S. Aird suggests 836 million. The official Chinese statements vary between 750 million and 900 million, the higher figure being rarer.[16]

We have no means of choosing among these divergent estimates. For the sake of convenience and conformity with the rest of this study, we will use the UN figures (see Table 9). In 1970 the population of China was 21.4 percent of the world population and 30.5 percent of all less developed countries. The dependency ratio was 661 per thousand. People under 20 years of age represented 45 percent of the population. The level of urbanization was rather low (21.7 percent versus 37.4 percent for the entire world and 25.0 percent for less developed countries). Citing five-year-average figures for the period 1970–1975, life expectancy

[15]While at first the 1953 census was thought to have been overestimated (a population under 500 million had been expected, yet the census gave a figure of 583 million), it is generally admitted today that the figure for 1953 was, if anything, underestimated. The sex ratio alone indicates that there was a significant underestimation of the female population. (Barring calamities, the sex ratio—the number of males per 100 females—is about the same for any given population.)

[16]It should be noted that the figures given correspond to different dates. One of the most valuable figures is Edgar Snow's: "In January 1971, I asked Chou En-lai if one could say that the Chinese population had now reached 800 million. After a minute, he told me: 'No, not yet, at all.'" (Snow, *La Longue Révolution*, Paris, Ed. Stock, 1973, p. 660.)

TABLE 8
Demographic Indicators for the Chinese Population in 1970

Sources	Total Population*	Birthrate†	Death Rate†	Natural Increase Rate†
L. Orleans	788	32	16	16
J. S. Aird	836	37.3	15.0	22.3
UN	772	27	10	17

*In millions.
†Per thousand.
SOURCES: See footnote 13. Since China's population in 1970 is an estimate, different assumptions of the evolution since 1953 produce different results. We will confine ourselves to the medium variant of the various sources.

was 61.6 years for men and 63.3 years for women, the total fertility rate was 3.8 per woman, the birthrate 26.9 per thousand, the death rate 10.3 per thousand, and the natural increase rate 16.6 per thousand.

In projecting China's demographic future, the key question is the evolution of fertility rates. In this regard, there is both a certainty and an uncertainty. The certainty is that, ignoring the severe fluctuations in what might be called the "population policy" of China, there has been since 1956, when an office for limiting births was created, an open effort to limit fertility.[17] Family planning is encouraged by the public authorities. While many different methods (contraceptives, abortion, sterilization) are used for limiting births, raising the marital age is considered the most effective instrument for slowing population growth. "The minimum legal age for marriage is 18, but Chairman Mao has asked that women postpone marriage until at least the age

[17]In May 1957, the Minister of Health declared: "If, without family planning, population is bound to grow, such growth prevents our nation from escaping rapidly from poverty and from becoming prosperous and powerful." The commentator of the time expresses this in one phrase, "The limitation of births, judged as a bad herb, is in fact a perfumed flower." See, for instance, Aird, "Population Policy and Demographic Prospects," p. 242.

TABLE 9
China—Selected Demographic Indicators, 1950–2000

	1950	1955	1960	1965	1970	1975	1980	1985	1990	1995	2000
Medium variant											
1. Population, total (1,000s)	558,190	605,081	654,488	710,324	771,840	838,803	907,609	973,155	1,031,142	1,089,572	1,147,987
2. Population, males (1,000s)	289,935	313,064	337,213	364,697	395,092	428,377	462,470	494,699	522,803	550,968	578,940
3. Population, females (1,000s)	268,255	292,017	317,276	345,626	376,748	410,426	445,139	478,456	508,339	538,604	569,047
4. Population ages 0–4 (% of total)	13.6	14.7	13.3	12.7	12.3	12.0	11.4	10.4	9.2	8.9	8.6
5. Population ages 5–14 (% of total)	20.6	21.3	23.5	23.6	22.2	21.4	21.1	20.6	19.6	17.9	16.7
6. Population ages 15–64 (% of total)	60.3	59.1	58.2	58.6	60.2	61.0	61.7	62.8	64.6	66.2	67.3
7. Population ages 65+ (% of total)	5.5	5.0	4.9	5.1	5.4	5.6	5.9	6.2	6.5	6.9	7.4
8. Population ages under 20 (% of total)	43.4	45.0	45.6	45.9	45.1	43.3	42.0	40.5	38.4	36.1	34.0
9. Women ages 15–49 (% of all women)	49.3	47.7	46.5	46.7	48.4	49.4	50.2	51.2	52.8	54.2	54.4
10. Dependency ratios (per 1,000)	658.6	693.5	718.0	706.0	660.7	640.5	621.6	592.7	548.0	509.5	485.2
11. Child-woman ratios (per 1,000)	572.9	638.6	590.6	557.8	518.5	495.8	463.1	413.9	355.0	332.9	320.2
12. Sex ratios (per 100 females)	108.1	107.2	106.3	105.5	104.9	104.4	103.9	103.4	102.8	102.3	101.7
13. Median ages (yr)	23.9	23.0	22.7	22.6	22.8	23.5	24.4	25.4	26.7	28.0	29.3
14. Urban population (% of total)	11.1	14.5	18.7	20.3	21.7	23.5	25.5	27.8	30.3	33.0	36.1
15. Population density (per km²)	58	63	68	74	80	87	95	101	107	114	120

	50–55	55–60	60–65	65–70	70–75	75–80	80–85	85–90	90–95	95–2,000
16. Rates of growth (%)	1.61	1.57	1.64	1.66	1.66	1.58	1.40	1.16	1.10	1.05
17. Natural increase rates (per 1,000)	16.1	15.7	16.4	16.6	16.6	15.8	13.9	11.6	11.0	10.4
18. Crude birthrates (per 1,000)	37.3	32.1	29.5	27.9	26.9	25.2	22.8	19.9	19.0	18.3
19. Crude death rates (per 1,000)	21.1	16.4	13.2	11.3	10.3	9.5	8.8	8.3	8.0	7.8
20. Gross reproduction rates	—	—	—	—	1.84	1.64	1.42	1.21	1.15	1.10
21. Net reproduction rates	—	—	—	—	1.61	1.47	1.30	1.13	1.09	1.06
22. Total fertility rates (per 1,000)	—	—	—	—	3772	3362	2911	2481	2358	2255

	1950	1955	1960	1965	1970	1975	1980	1985	1990	1995	2000
23. General fertility rates (per 1,000)	159.6	141.1	130.5	120.4	112.5	103.4	91.3	77.5	71.9	67.9	
24. Life expectancy, males (yr)	43.6	49.1	53.9	57.3	59.9	61.8	63.5	65.0	66.5	67.8	
25. Life expectancy, females (yr)	46.5	52.0	57.2	60.8	63.3	65.5	67.6	69.6	71.3	72.8	
26. Life expectancy, total (yr)	45.0	50.5	55.5	59.0	61.6	63.6	65.5	67.2	68.8	70.2	

High variant

	1950	1955	1960	1965	1970	1975	1980	1985	1990	1995	2000
1. Population, total (1,000s)	558,190	605,081	654,488	710,324	771,840	844,264	918,666	993,839	1,067,375	1,138,908	1,208,519
2. Population, males (1,000s)	289,935	313,064	337,213	364,697	395,092	431,157	468,094	505,216	541,214	576,023	609,663
3. Population, females (1,000s)	268,255	292,017	317,276	345,626	376,748	413,107	450,571	488,623	526,161	562,885	598,857
4. Population ages 0–4 (% of total)	13.6	14.7	13.3	12.7	12.3	12.5	11.9	11.2	10.4	9.7	9.1
5. Population ages 5–14 (% of total)	20.6	21.3	23.5	23.6	22.2	21.3	21.4	21.3	20.4	19.3	18.2
6. Population ages 15–64 (% of total)	60.3	59.1	58.2	58.6	60.2	60.6	60.9	61.5	62.9	64.3	65.6
7. Population ages 65+ (% of total)	5.5	5.0	4.9	5.1	5.4	5.6	5.8	6.0	6.3	6.6	7.0
8. Population ages under 20 (% of total)	43.4	45.0	45.6	45.9	45.1	43.6	42.7	41.7	40.5	38.4	36.4
9. Women ages 15–49 (% of all women)	49.3	47.7	46.5	46.7	48.4	49.1	49.6	50.2	51.5	52.9	53.4
10. Dependency ratios (per 1,000)	658.6	693.5	718.0	706.0	660.7	651.2	641.4	626.5	589.7	554.4	523.4
11. Child-woman ratios (per 1,000)	572.9	638.6	590.6	557.8	518.5	522.8	488.6	453.5	409.4	371.6	345.8
12. Sex ratios (per 100 females)	108.1	107.2	106.3	105.5	104.9	104.4	103.9	103.4	102.9	102.3	101.8
13. Median ages (yr)	23.9	23.0	22.7	22.6	22.8	23.3	24.1	24.8	25.6	26.6	27.8
14. Urban population (% of total)	11.1	14.5	18.7	20.3	21.7	23.8	26.2	29.1	32.4	36.2	40.5
15. Population density (per km²)	58	63	68	74	80	88	96	104	111	119	126

	50–55	55–60	60–65	65–70	70–75	75–80	80–85	85–90	90–95	95–2,000
16. Rates of growth (%)	1.61	1.57	1.64	1.66	1.79	1.69	1.57	1.43	1.30	1.19
17. Natural increase rates (per 1,000)	16.1	15.7	16.4	16.6	17.9	16.9	15.7	14.3	13.0	11.9
18. Crude birthrates (per 1,000)	37.3	32.1	29.5	27.9	28.3	26.4	24.5	22.5	20.8	19.4
19. Crude death rates (per 1,000)	21.1	16.4	13.2	11.3	10.3	9.5	8.8	8.2	7.8	7.5
20. Gross reproduction rates	—	—	—	—	1.94	1.73	1.56	1.42	1.30	1.20
21. Net reproduction rates	—	—	—	—	1.70	1.55	1.43	1.33	1.23	1.15

53

TABLE 9 (Continued)
China—Selected Demographic Indicators, 1950–2000

	1950	1955	1960	1965	1970	1975	1980	1985	1990	1995	2000
Medium variant											
22. Total fertility rates (per 1,000)	—	—	—	—	3977	3547	3198	2911	2665	2460	
23. General fertility rates (per 1,000)	159.6	141.1	130.5	120.4	118.6	109.1	100.1	89.8	80.6	73.8	
24. Life expectancy, males (yr)	43.6	49.1	53.9	57.3	59.9	61.8	63.5	65.0	66.5	67.8	
25. Life expectancy, females (yr)	46.5	52.0	57.2	60.8	63.3	65.5	67.6	69.6	71.3	72.8	
26. Life expectancy, total (yr)	45.0	50.5	55.5	59.0	61.6	63.6	65.5	67.2	68.8	70.2	

	1950	1955	1960	1965	1970	1975	1980	1985	1990	1995	2000
Low variant											
1. Population, total (1,000s)	558,190	605,081	654,488	710,324	771,840	829,344	883,439	932,576	980,792	1,027,950	1,072,819
2. Population, males (1,000s)	289,935	313,064	337,213	364,697	395,092	423,585	450,353	474,479	498,042	521,051	542,807
3. Population, females (1,000s)	268,255	292,017	317,276	345,626	376,748	405,758	433,086	458,097	482,750	506,900	530,011
4. Population ages 0–4 (% of total)	13.6	14.7	13.3	12.7	12.3	11.1	10.1	9.2	8.8	8.5	8.1
5. Population ages 5–14 (% of total)	20.6	21.3	23.5	23.6	22.2	21.7	20.6	19.1	17.6	16.5	16.0
6. Population ages 15–64 (% of total)	60.3	59.1	58.2	58.6	60.2	61.6	63.3	65.4	66.8	67.8	68.2
7. Population ages 65+ (% of total)	5.5	5.0	4.9	5.1	5.4	5.7	6.0	6.4	6.8	7.2	7.7
8. Population ages under 20 (% of total)	43.4	45.0	45.6	45.9	45.1	42.7	40.5	38.1	35.5	33.5	31.9
9. Women ages 15–49 (% of all women)	49.3	47.7	46.5	46.7	48.4	49.9	51.5	53.4	54.5	55.2	54.5
10. Dependency ratios (per 1,000)	658.6	693.5	718.0	706.0	660.7	623.3	580.7	529.8	496.3	475.7	466.7
11. Child-woman ratios (per 1,000)	572.9	638.6	590.6	557.8	518.5	452.8	400.4	350.2	327.4	310.9	299.9
12. Sex ratios (per 100 females)	108.1	107.2	106.3	105.5	104.9	104.4	104.0	103.6	103.2	102.8	102.4
13. Median ages (yr)	23.9	23.0	22.7	22.6	22.8	23.7	25.1	26.6	28.1	29.5	31.1
14. Urban population (% of total)	11.1	14.5	18.7	20.3	21.7	23.2	24.8	26.5	28.2	30.0	31.9
15. Population density (per km²)	58	63	68	74	80	86	92	97	102	107	112

	50–55	55–60	60–65	65–70	70–75	75–80	80–85	85–90	90–95	95–2,000
16. Rates of growth (%)	1.61	1.57	1.64	1.66	1.44	1.26	1.08	1.01	0.94	0.85
17. Natural increase rates (per 1,000)	16.1	15.7	16.4	16.6	14.4	12.6	10.8	10.1	9.4	8.5
18. Crude birthrates (per 1,000)	37.3	32.1	29.5	27.9	24.8	22.3	20.0	18.9	18.0	17.1
19. Crude death rates (per 1,000)	21.1	16.4	13.2	11.3	10.4	9.7	9.1	8.8	8.6	8.5
20. Gross reproduction rates	—	—	—	—	1.70	1.42	1.19	1.10	1.05	1.02
21. Net reproduction rates	—	—	—	—	1.47	1.26	1.08	1.02	0.98	0.97
22. Total fertility rates (per 1,000)	—	—	—	—	3485	2911	2440	2255	2153	2091
23. General fertility rates (per 1,000)	159.6	141.1	130.5	120.4	103.0	89.7	77.5	71.2	66.7	63.1
24. Life expectancy, males (yr)	43.6	49.1	53.9	57.3	59.4	61.4	63.1	64.7	66.2	67.5
25. Life expectancy, females (yr)	46.5	52.0	57.2	60.8	62.7	64.7	66.6	68.3	69.7	71.0
26. Life expectancy, total (yr)	45.0	50.5	55.5	59.0	61.0	63.0	64.8	66.5	67.9	69.2

SOURCE: UN, *World Demographic Indicators*, p. 99.

of 23 and men until after 26."[18] This represents a rather significant change in traditional behavior, as can be seen by the fact that the marital age in 1930 was about 15 or 16 years. After 1956, an intense propaganda campaign in favor of smaller families was carried out in work groups. Everything was done to minimize sexual stimulation. Premarital relationships were banned. What was original about this Chinese attitude was that limiting births was sought less in order to achieve economic and demographic equilibrium than to protect the health of mothers and children.

How effective Chinese birth control policies will be in the future remains to be seen. From 1954 to 1970 the national growth rate was notably higher than 2 percent, according to J. S. Aird; close to 1.6 percent, according to the UN calculation; and somewhere in between, with a clear decreasing trend (from 2.1 percent in 1954 to 1.6 percent in 1970), according to L. Orleans. Everything seems to indicate that there will be a rapid decrease in fertility in the future, but contradictions between the different statistical sources prevent accurate estimates of its extent. For example, it is generally thought that the model of the smaller family (two or three children) has tended to gain acceptance throughout the country (allowing for regional differences, which remain rather marked), but that the desire by families to have a son remains strong and serves to impede a decline in fertility.

This lack of information about family-planning effectiveness and the fact that the present age structure of the Chinese population is not known brings great uncertainty to any forecast. All that can be done is to make estimates on the basis of the age structure as set forth in the 1953 census and then make projections according to different hypotheses of fertility and mortality. How to decide which hypotheses are most probable is, as we have said, uncertain.

Aird has made estimates of the evolution of the Chinese population between 1953 and 1990 using four hypothetical models of fertility and mortality. For fertility, the most delicate problem,

[18]A. Faundes and T. Lukkainen, "Health and Family Planning Services in the Chinese People's Republic," *Studies in Family Planning*, vol. 3, no. 7, 1972. It is useful to mention, however, the two long periods of interruption of 1958–1962 and 1966–1969.

the models were designed on the basis of fertility levels observed on Taiwan at different periods of time, taking into account both the cultural similarities of the two populations and the earliest, strongest reductions in fertility on Taiwan.

Model 1 assumes a decline in intrinsic fertility rates patterned on the trend of intrinsic fertility in Taiwan since 1952 and a decline in mortality patterned on the trend in expectation of life at birth in Taiwan since 1946, the year in which the officially reported levels for Taiwan approximate the level estimated for 1970 in the series for the People's Republic of China. Model 2 is also based on the fertility and mortality trends for Taiwan, but the rate of decline in both parameters is only two-thirds as rapid as for Taiwan. Model 3 assumes that fertility and mortality decline at one-third the rates for Taiwan. Model 4 assumes constant intrinsic fertility and mortality levels for 1970 through 1990.[19]

As Table 10 illustrates, according to each of Aird's hypotheses, the Chinese population will grow by about 500 million people between 1970 and 1990 to a total of about 1.3 billion. The differences in results obtained using the four hypotheses are relatively small, which can be explained by the fact that the models assume a direct correlation between fertility and mortality. As a result, over the course of the period under consideration, every eventual reduction in fertility is offset by a lengthening of life expectancy. Yet by the end of the period, the decline in fertility begins to produce some effects—especially, of course, in models 1 and 2. Aird draws the following conclusions about the probable evolution of the population:

Even a major and successful effort at fertility reduction in the PRC is not likely to make much difference either in the size of the total population or in the size of the younger age groups; hence it cannot afford much relief from population pressure in general or from such specific problems as the need for education, employment, housing, and other services for young people.[20]

He goes on to say that efforts to decrease fertility will not be

[19]Aird, *Population Policy and Demographic Prospects*, p. 327.
[20]Ibid., p. 329.

TABLE 10
Estimates and Projections of the Population and Vital Rates of the People's
Republic of China 1953–1990
Population Figures in Thousands as of July 1; Vital Rates per 1,000 Population

Year	Population	Birth-rate	Death rate	Natural increase rate
1953	582,603	45.0	22.5	22.5
1955	610,881	44.0	19.5	24.5
1960	688,811	39.9	20.1	19.8
1965	750,532	37.2	16.5	20.7
1970	836,036	37.3	16.0	22.3
Projection model 1				
1970	836,036	37.3	15.0	22.3
1971	855,170	37.4	14.4	23.0
1972	875,283	37.4	13.9	23.5
1973	895,321	37.3	13.3	24.0
1974	918,236	37.2	12.8	24.3
1975	940,983	36.9	12.3	24.6
1976	964,462	36.4	11.7	24.7
1977	988,566	35.9	11.2	24.7
1978	1,013,151	35.1	10.6	24.5
1979	1,038,063	34.2	10.1	24.1
1980	1,063,159	33.2	9.6	23.7
1981	1,088,317	32.2	9.1	23.1
1982	1,113,435	31.1	8.6	22.5
1983	1,138,406	30.0	8.2	21.8
1984	1,163,122	28.9	7.7	21.1
1985	1,187,490	27.7	7.4	20.4
1986	1,211,429	26.6	7.1	19.6
1987	1,234,842	25.5	6.8	18.7
1988	1,257,643	24.5	6.6	17.9
1989	1,279,806	23.5	6.4	17.1
1990	1,301,260	22.4	6.2	16.2
Projection model 2				
1970	836,036	37.3	15.0	22.3
1971	855,107	37.4	14.6	22.8
1972	875,034	37.5	14.3	23.3
1973	895,783	37.5	13.9	23.6
1974	917,348	37.5	13.6	23.9
1975	939,705	37.4	13.2	24.2
1976	962,815	37.2	12.8	24.4

TABLE 10 (Continued)
Estimates and Projections of the Population and Vital Rates of the People's
Republic of China 1953–1990
Population Figures in Thousands as of July 1; Vital Rates per 1,000 Population

Year	Population	Birth-rate	Death rate	Natural increase rate
1977	986,587	36.9	12.5	24.4
1978	1,010,921	36.4	12.1	24.3
1979	1,035,728	35.8	11.7	24.2
1980	1,060,905	35.2	11.3	23.9
1981	1,036,386	34.5	10.9	23.6
1982	1,112,097	33.7	10.5	23.2
1983	1,137,958	33.0	10.2	22.8
1984	1,163,940	32.2	9.9	22.4
1985	1,189,971	31.4	9.6	21.9
1986	1,215,983	30.7	9.3	21.4
1987	1,241,963	30.0	9.1	20.9
1988	1,267,881	29.3	8.9	20.4
1989	1,293,678	28.6	8.7	19.9
1990	1,319,342	28.0	8.6	19.4
Projection model 3				
1970	836,036	37.3	15.0	22.3
1971	855,031	37.5	14.8	22.6
1972	874,741	37.6	14.7	22.9
1973	895,178	37.8	14.5	23.2
1974	916,374	37.9	14.4	23.6
1975	938,323	38.0	14.2	23.8
1976	960,988	38.0	14.0	24.0
1977	984,353	37.9	13.8	24.1
1978	1,008,360	37.8	13.6	24.1
1979	1,032,942	37.5	13.4	24.1
1980	1,058,042	37.2	13.2	23.9
1981	1,083,583	36.8	13.0	23.8
1982	1,109,579	36.4	12.8	23.6
1983	1,135,985	36.0	12.6	23.4
1984	1,162,754	35.5	12.4	23.2
1985	1,189,880	35.1	12.2	23.0
1986	1,217,372	34.7	12.0	22.7
1987	1,245,188	34.3	11.8	22.5
1988	1,273,330	33.9	11.7	22.2
1989	1,301,818	33.6	11.6	22.0
1990	1,330,648	33.3	11.5	21.8

TABLE 10 (Continued)
Estimates and Projections of the Population and Vital Rates of the People's
Republic of China 1953–1990
Population Figures in Thousands as of July 1; Vital Rates per 1,000 Population

Year	Population	Birth-rate	Death rate	Natural increase rate
Projection model 4				
1970	836,036	37.3	15.0	22.3
1971	854,943	37.5	15.1	22.4
1972	874,415	37.7	15.1	22.6
1973	894,504	38.0	15.2	22.8
1974	915,254	38.3	15.2	23.0
1975	936,695	38.6	15.3	23.3
1976	958,834	38.8	15.3	23.5
1977	981,663	39.0	15.4	23.6
1978	1,005,156	39.1	15.4	23.7
1979	1,029,281	39.1	15.4	23.7
1980	1,054,008	39.1	15.4	23.7
1981	1,079,310	39.1	15.4	23.7
1982	1,105,178	39.1	15.4	23.7
1983	1,131,609	39.0	15.4	23.9
1984	1,158,600	38.9	15.4	23.9
1985	1,186,159	38.8	15.3	23.5
1986	1,214,300	38.7	15.3	23.4
1987	1,243,046	38.7	15.3	23.4
1988	1,272,422	38.6	15.3	23.3
1989	1,302,441	38.5	15.2	23.3
1990	1,333,128	38.5	15.2	23.3

SOURCE: Aird, *Population Policy and Demographic Prospects,* pp. 328–329.

really successful until the death rate declines significantly, presumably because people will not want to have fewer children if they think a large proportion of them are likely to die:

What these models suggest is that, barring catastrophe or spectacular changes in contraceptive technology and in the means of political coercion, even the most successful family limitation effort is not likely to provide much relief from population pressure in the PRC until mortality has completed its transition to the lower levels characteristic of developed countries. On the other hand, the failure to make significant progress in family limitation while continuing to reduce mortality levels can only increase the rate of population growth in the short run and the severity of the attendant population problems. Taking into account the experiences of the three birth control campaigns and the implications of the population models, there is no reason to expect any great change in China's demographic prospects in the immediate future.[21]

Aird's calculations are quite different from the UN data: according to the UN's medium variant, the population will reach 1.03 billion by 1990 and the age structure will change slightly, but the death rate and especially the birthrate will be markedly reduced, respectively, to 8 and 19 per thousand in 1990–1995. Life expectancy will be increased substantially, to 66.5 years for men and 71.3 years for women. These discrepancies in projections underline the level of uncertainty involved in analyzing the Chinese population. It is difficult to choose between them.[22] On the one hand, Aird's calculations seem to be exaggerated. The base population figure he uses is higher than the most plausible and generally accepted maximum level for 1970. His growth hypotheses are very high (rates above 2 percent per year, except for the last years in variants 1 and 2) in view of the abrupt slowdown in the birthrate after the Cultural Revolution. The official goal was to reduce the growth rate to less than 2 percent, and it seems that such a rate has now been attained. But if Aird perhaps errs by overestimating the size and growth of the population, the UN medium variant perhaps appears too optimistic. If the most accurate figure for the end of 1975 is 880 to 900 million, there would have to be an abrupt decline in birthrates to produce the UN's estimate of only 1.03 billion people 15 years hence, since the passage by the age groups born during the 1960s into the period of maximum fertility would otherwise cause a marked increase in the population.

[21]Ibid.

[22]As Leo Orleans put it before providing his own estimates: "The differences between the UN and FDAD [J. S. Aird's] estimates obviously boil down to a divergence in the interpretation of a whole range of demographic, socioeconomic, and political developments in China during the past two decades." (L. Orleans, "China's Population Figures," *Studies in Family Planning*, vol. 7, no. 2, February 1976, p. 54.)

TWO

The Main Issues of the 1980s

Demographic and related social problems around the world will be most greatly aggravated if the most pessimistic of the various population projections come true, but in any case major problems will arise. For summary purposes, we can identify six pressing issues that will be linked to demographic growth in the course of the 1980s:

1. Population structures: pension costs and educational costs
2. Some aspects of urbanization and town planning
3. Economic costs of demographic fluctuations
4. Internal population distribution and the problem of minorities
5. Geopolitical balances among nations
6. Demographic pressure and international migration

We have excluded from this presentation certain major problems that are linked to demographic trends but are largely tangential to demographic analysis, such as the continuing inadequacy of the food supply, which will remain one of the major causes of high mortality levels in certain countries.

POPULATION STRUCTURE

As we noted earlier, in the next 10 or 20 years the numerical relationships of age groups to each other within populations will scarcely be affected (except at the base of the age pyramids), no matter what growth hypothesis is used. If we take, for example, Frejka's calculations,[1] we can see that in 1985, according to his projections P1 and P2, the proportion of persons over 65 in the developed countries will have increased to 11.6 and 11.8 percent, respectively, from 10.8 percent in 1970, i.e., a variation of less than 1 percent. In the less developed countries, according to projections P4 and P5, the increase is from 3.4 percent in 1970 to 3.6 percent in 1985, a negligible change. However, in the developed countries at least, such a demographic variation may have important economic consequences.

In those developed countries where the pensions of retired people are paid for by the earnings of people still working, the rate of contribution necessary to keep the system fiscally sound depends basically on the ratio of retired people to working people, also taking into account a working person's average salary. A decrease in the number of working people compared with retirees or a reduction in the average salary leads inevitably to an increase in the contribution rates. In addition, in countries such as France, where different sectors of the working force—farmers, business people, salaried employees, etc.—have separate pension systems, changes associated with economic growth in the different sectors pose the problem of financial equilibrium for each sector. However, it is probable that the increasing entry of women into the labor force during the 1980s will enable the system to continue functioning at an acceptable cost.

In the less developed countries, problems arise at the other extreme of the age spectrum. To the degree that fertility remains high the costs of education will be increased, and even under the most favorable circumstances educational needs will weigh heavily on the economies of these countries. Moreover, even if fertility is lowered, a reduction in educational costs will not be felt before a decade's time. During the last few years in the less developed countries there have been considerable increases in the proportion of the population in school. UNESCO attributes this principally to an increased population growth rate, decolonization, and the democratization of education.

[1]Tomas Frejka, *The Future of Population Growth: Alternative Paths to Equilibrium*, John Wiley & Sons, New York, 1973. See a further discussion of Frejka on pp. 77–78 of this essay.

If one considers, on the one hand, the gap between the developed and less developed countries with respect to the number of persons in school and, on the other hand, the gap even within less developed countries between the number of boys and the number of girls in school, one can expect that the demand for education will continue to grow. A considerable effort to train teachers will be required. Thus there will most likely be an increase in the cost of education to be borne by the labor force, and it is by no means certain that the countries involved will be able to meet the demand. Under these conditions it may be difficult to maintain the quality of educational systems whose current inadequacies already impose a high economic cost on their countries. Nonetheless, education should remain a high-priority objective, because it seems to be one of the most effective instruments in reducing fertility. There appears to exist a rather close relationship between a minimum of five to six years' education and the size of families. However, progress in education might accelerate migratory movements and aggravate urbanization problems. In any case, educational problems are going to constitute one of the major worries for the less developed countries in the coming decades, and the evolution of the population will play a major role in alleviating or aggravating them. Thus, a group of UNESCO experts have written, "Looking at the future, the capacity of many countries to finance the planned expansion of their educational systems seems to depend on whether or not they manage to curb the rate of population growth which considerably exceeds that upon which their plans are based."[2]

SOME ASPECTS OF URBANIZATION

Continued urbanization will probably dictate the creation of new towns. While in the short run a new town is the immediate solution to the concentration of population, in the long run the demographic structures of new towns will change, just as they changed in older urban settlements, and these towns will then

[2]UNESCO, *Population and Education*, paper for World Population Conference, Bucharest, 1974 (E/CONF60/CBP/20).

have their own problems of matching housing supply and demand.

In the case of the developed countries, new towns are created at the outset by a group whose age structure is significantly different from the population of the country as a whole: there are more young children and adults between 25 and 45 years and far fewer adolescents, youths, older adults, and aged persons. Let us suppose that, for this population, death and fertility rates are comparable to those observed in developed countries over the past few years (i.e., 2.2 children per woman, average life expectancy at birth of around 71), and in order to simplify things, let us also suppose that all the new inhabitants who are going to have more children will do so within a 10-year period. What will happen to the population? A simple model shows the following results.[3] At the beginning, because of the age structure of the settler population, there will be a high growth rate in spite of fertility being near the replacement level. Thus, in 20 years' time the population will have increased by about 50 percent. By this time, too, the children who came to the town with their settler parents will have entered the reproductive cycle and births will once again increase. The population as a whole will be older, and the proportion of people on pensions, initially few or non-existent, will grow very rapidly, then stabilize after some moderate fluctuations.

But we still ought to examine a consideration that was, understandably, the reason for creating the new town in the first place, namely, the problem of matching the housing needs of the population with its family structure. If we consider not the total size of the population but the problem of matching households with houses, there are two possibilities: the children will either live in new housing in the same new town or will leave the new town and move to another area. (It is unrealistic to assume that they will be housed with their parents.) What about the parents? Either all the original settlers and their families will stay in the

[3]H. Le Bras and J. C. Chesnais, "Cycle de l'Habitat et l'Age des Habitants," *Population*, no. 2, March–April 1976, pp. 269–299.

town for life, and all housing will remain occupied until the last surviving member of every household dies, or the families will not all remain in the town throughout their lives. In the former case, there will be the problem of constructing new housing for these families of the original settlers, assuming the existence of free space; the population as a whole will age, and the school-age population will decline. In the latter case, population structure will be influenced by emigration—and presumably by immigration, if new residents move in to take the places of those who moved out. Whatever the outcome, the sociodemographic balances of work, health, and education in the town will be altered. And calculations demonstrate that an optimum balance between population and housing will be reestablished only after another 100 years.

In the case of the less developed countries, as a consequence of a higher rate of population growth in new towns, a higher death rate, and a more flexible environment, the difficulties are fundamentally different. The high fertility, high levels of internal migration, unequal distribution of income, and low rate of capital accumulation characteristic of these countries render rather hypothetical the likelihood that the urban population's needs will be met. There are simply too many people involved, too much to be done, and no way to mobilize the necessary resources to do it. The difficulty is increased by the fact that any efforts to improve the urban environment increase the appeal of cities to country dwellers and thus risk nullifying themselves.

THE ECONOMIC COSTS OF DEMOGRAPHIC FLUCTUATIONS

While it is normal in looking at demographic projections to pay greatest attention to continuing trends in population growth, the fluctuations of demographic indicators during the 20-year period we are examining should not be neglected. We should emphasize that fluctuations will appear not only if there are reversals in fertility trends—something that is not unlikely in the developed countries—but also, paradoxically, if fertility rates remain constant. In the latter case, the population will in the long run achieve a stable structure, but the path to that stability will involve fluctuations during the transitional period. Stability will of necessity be achieved slowly, since there is a limit to how quickly human behavior and the circumstances of human life can change. In any case, these fluctuations, especially the variations in the percentage of the population in school, can have a rather significant economic effect, as studies have shown for both the less developed countries and the developed countries.[4]

In Mexico, for example, suppose that the growth rate were to diminish progressively to attain 0 in 1995–2000, that fertility would fluctuate between 0.6 children per woman in 1995–2000 (the lowest point) and 3.8 children per woman in 2040–2045 (the highest point), and that the school-age population would fluctuate between 2 million and 7.2 million, the stabilized level being 4.6 million.[5]

A very brief explanation of these fluctuations would be as follows: The abrupt drop in fertility would reduce very perceptibly the cohorts of girls under 14 in the first years of the projection. A few decades later, these girls would reach childbearing age, and the birthrate would decline very markedly. But since the death rate would be growing very perceptibly because of the aging of the population in the first years of the projection, in order for the growth rate to remain 0 the birthrate, from that time on, would have to compensate for this by once again becoming very high. Thus there would be fluctuations.

---

[4]Besides Frejka, *Future of Population Growth*, see, for Mexico, J. Bourgeois-Pichat and Si Ahmed Taleb, ``Un Taux d'Acroissement Nul pour les Pays en Voie de Développement en l'An 2000. Rêve ou Réalité?'' *Population*, no. 5, September–October 1970, pp. 957–974. For France, see H. Le Bras and G. Tapinos, *Les Perspectives Démographiques à Long Terme et Leurs Conséquences: Communication au Colloque Franco-Sovietique sur les Méthodes de Planification et de Prévision à Long Terme*, working papers, Institut National d'Études Démographiques, Paris, October 1975.

[5]These projections for Mexico are made by Bourgeois-Pichat and Taleb in ``Taux d'Accroissement Nul.''

INTERNAL POPULATION DISTRIBUTION AND THE PROBLEM OF MINORITIES

In the countries with a heterogeneous ethnic composition and where group differences in demographic behavior and socioeconomic conditions are significant, the relative distribution of the different groups may undergo changes that could upset today's unstable equilibrium. Unfortunately, we do not for the most part have sufficient data on ethnic distribution within countries and so it is difficult to take the phenomenon fully into account, even though there is no doubt about overall trends. We can only provide certain illustrations here.

A very sketchy typology distinguishes countries in which there is (1) a dominant majority, (2) a dominant minority, or (3) a division of the population into two major groups.

According to Frejka,[6] the Jewish population of Israel, a country of the first type, was about 2.4 million in 1970 and will reach 3.0 million in 1990 (projection P2), while the non-Jewish population, which was 0.3 million in 1970, will reach 0.7 million by 1990 (projections P3, P4, and P5). In other words, the Jewish people will be proportionately reduced from 87 percent of the Israeli population in 1970 to no more than 81 percent in 1990. The relative variation is not perhaps very great, but it is nevertheless not insignificant.

In the Soviet Union, which has a dominant Russian majority, the very differing demographic evolutions of its constituent republics have produced a marked increase in the size of the non-Russian ethnic populations, a trend that is expected to continue during the next decades and that the policy of "Russification" appears powerless to check. In 1972 the birthrates were 15.3 per thousand in the Russian Soviet Federated Socialist Republic—largest of the 15 republics, stretching across Europe and Siberia, predominantly Russian; 15.5 per thousand in the Ukraine; 23.5 per thousand in Kazakhstan; and 33.2 per thousand in Uzbek-

[6]Frejka, reference tables to *The Future of Population Growth,* Population Council, New York, 1973.

istan. As Mme. Carrère d'Encausse emphasizes, the demographic evolution of the various ethnic groups risks upsetting the economic and political balance of the U.S.S.R.[7]

Belgium illustrates the effect of differential demographic evolution in a country of the third type, formerly made up about half and half of two ethnic groups. In 1900 the French-speaking Walloons represented 40 percent of the total population, as against only 32 percent in 1970. A decline in birthrates, which began earlier and was more marked in Wallonia than in Flemish-speaking Flanders, has accentuated the aging of the Walloon population, whose growth since 1965 has been due only to foreign immigration. The language quarrel that is now the essential issue of Belgian politics cannot be attributed only to the specific demographic evolution of each region, but there is no doubt that it has played a major role in reversing traditional Walloon economic, political, and cultural domination. Demographic trends indicate for the future a consolidation of the present situation.

The case of Lebanon, another country of the third type, is particularly interesting to the extent that any asynchronous evolution in fertility of the Muslim and Christian populations will compromise an already unstable equilibrium. As was mentioned earlier, adequate data are not available, but according to a CICRED monograph published in 1974,[8] the birthrates were estimated at 25 per thousand and 42 per thousand for the Christian and Muslim groups, respectively, (the corresponding general fertility rates being 125 per thousand and 210 per thousand). The most recent information on the religious distribution of the population dates from 1943, when there were an estimated 47 percent Muslims and 53 percent Christians. It is rather likely that the Christian population has now become a minority and that its downward trend is going to continue through the 1980s.

As a last example, we will look at minority-dominated South Africa. According to the census of 1970, the South African population was 17.5 percent white, 9.4 percent colored, 2.9 percent

[7]H. Carrère d'Encausse, *Le Monde*, March 2, 1977.

[8]Y. Courbage and P. Fargues, *La Population du Liban*, CICRED Series, Publications de L'Université Libanaise, Beyrouth, 1974.

Asian, and 70.2 percent black. We do not have the data necessary to describe and analyze the different fertility rates for each racial group. However, just considering the differences in birthrates for these groups (white, 23.5 per thousand; colored, 36.2 per thousand; Asian, 32.7 per thousand; and black, 43 per thousand), we can get an idea of how accentuated the minority position of the white population will become by 1990—a development that will further aggravate the present tense situation.

THE GEOPOLITICAL BALANCE AMONG NATIONS

Assume for a moment that the economic development of the poor nations were to be sought so actively by the entire world community, particularly by the rich nations, that all the countries of the world would enjoy a similar standard of living. This may seem like a ridiculous formulation, since such a widespread re-distribution of wealth is not likely to occur in the near future, but it makes an important point. Even if this redistribution did occur, one important difference between countries would remain: size of population. While a country with a large population is not necessarily a powerful country (and one should not, in any case, confuse well-being with power), there is no example of a powerful country that has not had a large population relative to others. A large population has always been a necessary but not sufficient condition for power.

This may explain in part why less developed countries some-times resist population policies that seem indisputably rational to the developed countries. Aside from the rational difficulties developing countries face in determining the relationship be-tween demographic growth and improved socioeconomic con-ditions, their political choices sometimes seem to be motivated by considerations of a different nature, particularly in relation to the United States. Reasoning is frequently simplistic, taking the form of the following syllogism:

Proposition 1: The United States advises a restrictive policy.

Proposition 2: Any advice of the United States corresponds to its own interests and might be (or is necessarily) contrary to our interests.

Conclusion: We ought to reject restrictive policies.

As a Latin American demographer said: "The limitation of births? We do not know the demographic and economic effects, but because the Americans are for it, we are against it." This significant ideological aspect of the demographic future is generally underestimated. The 1974 population conference in Bucharest at least reminded us of it.[9]

Looking to the past for examples of the relation between power and population, we may cite the example of France, which constituted 15 percent of the European population at the beginning of the nineteenth century but because of subsequent reductions in fertility had only 8 percent of the population a century and a half later. And while France was undoubtedly a major power at the beginning of the period, it was no longer so at the end. If we examine the current populations of various regional groupings— for example, Brazil and Argentina, the countries of the Maghreb (Algeria, Tunisia, Morocco), or the Asian countries of China, India, and Pakistan—we note that any unilateral effort to limit birthrates will lead to a relative loss of population vis-à-vis neighbors.

Table 11 presents further comparisons of this type taken from UN projections. An exercise like this, though purely hypothetical, rests on reasonable assumptions that exclude certain comparisons. In view of the convergent evolution of demographic trends in the different developed countries, a comparison of, say, a high variant in France and a low one in Germany would be nonsense. On the contrary, in some cases—of which Table 11 gives examples—the possibility of divergent trends cannot be put aside. It is not the place here to argue that such divergent trends would create or aggravate international tensions, but if any of the hypothetical trends were to become reality, a balance of power would be altered.

[9]See the discussion of the Bucharest conference in Phyllis Piotrow's essay, pp. 97–100 of this volume.

TABLE 11
Comparison of Opposite Variants for Certain Countries or Groups of Countries

	Total Population (Millions)			Annual Growth Rates (Percent)	
	1975	1990	2000	1985–1990	1995–2000
United States (low variant)	213	239	251	0.70	0.41
Mexico (high variant)	59	100	141	3.55	3.32
Western Europe (low variant)	152	160	164	0.31	0.18
Northern Africa (high variant)	98	153	202	2.99	2.70
Israel (low variant)	3	4	5	1.35	1.06
Egypt, Syria, Jordan, Lebanon (high variant)	50	75	96		
China (low variant)	829	981	1,073	1.01	0.85
India (high variant)	613	900	1,124	2.47	2.10
India (low variant)	613	833	969	1.92	1.39
Bangladesh (high variant)	74	116	153	2.99	2.65
Greece (low variant)	9	9	10	0.31	0.22
Turkey (high variant)	40	60	77	2.68	2.40

SOURCE: UN, *Population Prospects as Assessed in 1973*, pp. 100–105.

DEMOGRAPHIC PRESSURE AND INTERNATIONAL MIGRATION

The last two decades have witnessed one of the major migration movements in world history, comparable in numbers with the great transoceanic migrations of the nineteenth century and the years preceeding the First World War. The causes of migration in the last 20 years have been mainly economic and institutional, and projections cannot be evaluated in the same way as they can be for fertility or mortality. It is necessary to predict economic trends before making any guess about migratory movements. Nevertheless, one may question whether demographic pressure in some countries may be strong enough to cause migration to less populated countries.

The economic hardships imposed on everyone—particularly the less developed countries—by the oil crisis have initiated a new phase in international migrations. It is clear that in the coming years migration policies will be highly restrictive. Will the demographic pressure exerted by some less developed countries be strong enough to overcome restrictive immigration policies? In the next two decades, at least, the increase of the labor force in the developed countries will probably impede legal immigration, but we have to expect an increase in illegal immigration. The conflict between the right to migrate and the right of countries to control migration may lead in some cases to severe tensions in international relations.

THE LONG-TERM FUTURE OF THE WORLD POPULATION

Our description of the demographic situation in 1990 would be insufficient if it were limited to a cross-sectional analysis of demographic indicators for that year alone. A projection is like the picture of a car traveling at a certain speed that an observer, placed along the road, sees at a given point in time. The demographic situation in 1990 as we have described it will be the result of an ineluctable evolutionary pattern that no demographic policy, however coercive, can alter in such a brief period of time. By way of conclusion, then, it may be useful to emphasize those elements of the "speed" our car will attain.

We have seen that through the year 1990 the growth rates of the world's population and of its various components will have no noteworthy effect on the age structure and, in particular, on the proportion of people in the labor force. Yet beyond 1990, the effects of a reduction in fertility on the aging of the population will be felt and will cause very important structural changes.

A long-term perspective on world population underscores three fundamental questions, the answers to which are necessary for an assessment of the future evolution and well-being of humanity:

1. Is the stabilization of demographic growth *desirable*?
2. If so, within what time frame would it be *technically possible*?
3. What is the *probability* of such an objective being reached in such a time frame?

To the first question, the response is emphatic. Certainly there are countries, indeed entire regions, in which there is no over-population problem, and they might still be able to support a rather large increase in their population without any ill effects on the well-being of their inhabitants; but if one looks at the situation for the entire world, the stabilization of population growth is an imperative.

To what degree is such stabilization technically possible?[10] Attaining stabilization, i.e., a zero rate of population growth in the immediate future, is objectively impossible because human behavior and the circumstances of human life simply cannot change that fast. The only technically possible objective is to aim for a reduction of the net reproduction rate to the replacement level by some reasonable target date, perhaps the year 2000 for most less developed countries. If this ambitious goal could be

[10]This fundamental problem has been analyzed by Bourgeois-Pichat and Taleb in "Taux d'Acroissement Nul," and by Frejka in *Future of Population Growth*.

75

reached, it would still take several decades (say, until 2070) for the size of the population to become stabilized, and even then it would still be two or three times larger than it had been in 1970.

There still remains the last question and the most important one: What chance is there to reduce the net reproduction rate to 1 by the year 2000? Historical experience in the developed countries and still uncertain lessons drawn from changes that have occurred in some less developed countries bring out several factors that are both encouraging and discouraging. In addition there are certain exogenous elements of uncertainty about economic-demographic developments in the century to come which might either promote or prevent the achievement of the goal.

The question could be put this way: Should the theory of demographic transition, that is, the theory that economic and social development are a prerequisite to declining fertility, be considered as universally applicable or applicable only to certain societies? The theory of demographic transition postulates that not only socioeconomic development but also a decline in mortality are necessary preconditions to a reduction in fertility; that fertility declines slowly at the beginning, then accelerates, then slows down again; and that it stabilizes finally at the net replacement level. This theory was originally considered to be a coherent model for explaining the demographic evolution of the developed countries. Recent studies have demonstrated, however, that the theory does not always work in practice. Economic development has *not* always preceded a reduction in fertility, nor has reduced mortality. In addition, in a society in so-called natural equilibrium—in which death rates compensate for birthrates—the differences in fertility levels among different cultural groups seem greater than the differences in overall fertility levels between the phase of natural equilibrium and the phase of transition.

This recent examination of the logic behind the theory of demographic transition raises the question of the application of the theory to less developed countries. Certainly there are rather notable differences between the developed and less developed countries. In the latter, fertility levels are clearly higher than those observed in the European countries before the transition took place, and the potentials for growth are even higher. Yet it seems that after a reduction in fertility has begun in a less developed country, its rate is much more rapid than that observed in Europe.

When can we reasonably expect world population to stabilize? To review the different answers to this question Frejka has calculated five series of projections of world population according to the time period during which the net reproduction rate will reach the replacement level. The time when the population growth rate reaches 0 and thus the size of the population stabilizes is then deduced (see Table 12).

It is certain that the different projections are not equally probable for the developed countries and the less developed countries. The developed countries as a whole might reach a net reproduction rate of 1 around 1980–1985 (projection P2) or even before, which corresponds to a stabilization of the population by about the year 2095. If one takes 1970 as the base year (= 100), the

TABLE 12
Projections of World Population Depending Upon When the Net Reproduction Rate of 1 Is Reached

Projections	NRR* = 1	RPG = 0	N	IG
P1	1970–1975	2095–2100 (2010)	5,690	156
P2	1980–1985	2095–2100 (2020)	6,417	132
P3	2000–2005	2095–2100 (2030)	8,389	230
P4	2020–2025	2120–2125 (2045)	11,172	306
P5	2040–2045	2145–2150 (2060)	15,148	415

*NRR = net reproduction rate. RPG = rate of population growth. Under RPG, the time span in the left column indicates approximately when the population will be stabilized. The year in parentheses indicates approximately when the annual growth rate will drop below 0.5 percent. N = size of the population (in hundred thousands) in the year *italicized*. IG = index of growth, from base 1970 (= 100) to year of stabilization.

SOURCE: Frejka, *Future of Population Growth*, Reference Tables, pp. 18, 24, 28, 38.

total size of the population will stabilize at an index of 132. With respect to the less developed countries, uncertainties about the rate of change in fertility make the choice of the most probable projection more difficult. Projections P1 and P2 can be put aside as too optimistic; it can also be held, without denying the failures in present efforts to control births, that projection P5 is overly pessimistic. Two major hypotheses remain: the rather optimistic one (P3), according to which the net reproduction rate will reach the replacement level around the year 2000, the population will continue to grow for a century, and in the less developed countries will stabilize at a level around 2.7 times the size of the 1970 level; and the rather pessimistic projection (P4), according to which the net reproduction rate will fall to 1 only around 2020–2025 and stabilization will not be reached until around 2100, with the population of the less developed countries almost quadrupling in the meantime.

It is rather certain that in the developed countries a reduction in the net reproduction rate to the replacement level will be achieved several decades before it is achieved in the less developed countries; moreover, because of the differential age structure and higher growth potential of the less developed countries, the relative size of the developed countries in the world population is bound to become notably smaller. One cannot, however, push this type of comparison too far, since it presupposes that the classification of countries as developed and less developed will be the same at both ends of the time period, and it ignores cyclical reverses in fertility trends. But whatever the classification at the end of the period, the urgency of reducing the growth rate of the world population is clear.

No consensus can currently be reached on the question of whether the less developed countries will evolve along the same path as the developed countries. However, recent studies in historical demography and, more important, recent experience in family-planning programs suggest two conclusions. First, deliberate family-planning policies based on modern contraceptive devices become effective only after a spontaneous decline in fertility on the part of individuals has already begun; in other words, policies restricting births can accelerate but not initiate a reduction of fertility. Second, the changed attitudes of couples toward children which cause them to start practicing birth control are either encouraged or discouraged by the cultural structures that characterize a given population. Subcultural groupings within a single country can vary as widely as cultures in different countries. Thus there can be neither an a priori transposition of the theory of demographic transition from one country to another nor a pure and simple rejection of it for the less developed countries.

The uncertainty surrounding forecasts about the most likely time frame for stabilizing the world population, which the different hypotheses advanced on this subject suggest, makes such forecasts more wishful thinking than prediction, whether they are catastrophically pessimistic, like the *Limits to Growth* approach, or more optimistic, like the views of the UN. All we can say is that the vague declaration found in one of the official documents of the Bucharest conference that "the basic hypothesis is . . . that the stabilization of the world population can be realized in the foreseeable future" is as certain as we can be.

Population Policies for the 1980s: Meeting the Crest of the Demographic Wave

Phyllis T. Piotrow

ONE

Introduction

In the 1960s, as the subjects of population growth, fertility, and especially birth control emerged from the shadows of pervasive political taboo to become a legitimate field of government concern, the concept of population policy was revolutionized. In the late nineteenth and early twentieth centuries, several Western European governments had deliberately pursued pronatalist policies to boost their declining birthrates. But before the 1960s, the term *population policy*, if used at all, was applied mainly to immigration and declining fertility in Europe. Virtually all governments established immigration policies, whether to encourage or discourage would-be workers or citizens, as an early and basic expression of national sovereignty. Until the second half of the twentieth century, however, governments and demographers did not consider the possibility of national policies to promote lower fertility—not even in Asia, where the high fertility and dense population of "Mother India," for example, had always attracted attention. On the contrary, before the Second World War most governments prohibited all forms of artificial birth control as dangers to individual health or morals, but these restrictions were not viewed or adopted as population policies.

Governments began to change their attitudes with surprising rapidity after the war. In the late forties and early fifties, Japan, aware that its fast-growing population could no longer use military force to expand beyond its own island boundaries, legalized abortion, sterilization, and other forms of contraception. By the early 1960s, government leaders in India, Pakistan, China, Sweden, and finally the United States—influenced by 15 years of studies that showed world population was increasing dramatically—began to give the growth phenomenon serious attention.

The first governments actually to provide family-planning supplies and services were China, India, and Pakistan. Other developing countries soon followed suit, and by 1975 most of these countries had some type of government-supported contraceptive program. Moreover, they were receiving assistance from many of the developed countries, which were increasingly removing barriers to the availability of birth control supplies and information within their own borders.

These policies have, of course, been controversial in many countries, including the United States, because of organized opposition from the Roman Catholic Church and other traditionalist groups. In fact, it is church opposition, which first became vocal in the nineteenth century, that kept the issue of publicly supported birth control out of national policy debates in many developed countries for decades—even though most citizens were using some form of birth control. But in the 1960s, because it was becoming unavoidably clear that demographic developments were threatening the basic socioeconomic objectives of many countries, government intervention to control fertility was not to be stopped.

In response to current population policies—and perhaps also for other reasons—fertility rates have begun declining around the world, as the most recent available data suggest. But the decline is coming too late to prevent a major result of earlier high fertility from becoming a critical problem in the future: the one billion young adults who will be living in the developing countries by 1990. They will be the parents of the 1980s, and their decisions on family size will determine future demographic configurations. These young adults will also be the greatest participants in the already swelling migrations of developing-country populations from their own countries to more developed countries and from rural to urban areas within their own countries.

The strain of internal migration on housing, health facilities, schools, and other municipal resources; the need to provide training and jobs for semiskilled rural strangers in an urban environment; the potential for violence if their needs are not met—as well as the financial expense, administrative complexity, and political difficulty of many suggested solutions to internal migration problems—indicate that this may be a much tougher nut to crack than the fertility problem.

Although internal migration policies are still in their infancy—perhaps a decade behind family-planning policies in their definition, evaluation, and implementation—they are already an important component of development planning. It has become clear that factory jobs, minimum wages, subsidized-food programs, and other attractions that draw people to large cities, as well as the agricultural modernization that pushes them off the farms, are for all practical purposes population policies, although their explicit reasons for being are quite different.

It has also become clear that to reverse the trend and deflect migration from the cities will require strategies explicitly tailored to that goal. Strategies currently being discussed or practiced include job creation in rural areas, the use of labor-intensive rather than capital-intensive technologies, bonuses or other incentives to influence where people move, and withdrawal of ration cards or other disincentives to keep them from moving.

Of course, anything that makes life more rewarding where one is living acts as a brake on migration. Thus many of the policies that apply to internal migration could apply to international migration as well—although "guest worker" programs and other specific measures to manage international migration will also be necessary.

For the same reason, socioeconomic development generally is a very important element of migration policy (and indeed of fertility policy, as was proclaimed at the Bucharest World Population Conference in 1974). Whatever specific forms this development takes, it will require efficient government organization at the national level to deliver necessary services; wider involvement at the grass-roots level to make these services available and acceptable to the average citizen; and funds, research aid, and technical assistance from the developed world. These are all parts of an attempted population solution for the 1980s.

POSTWAR DEMOGRAPHIC CHANGE

The sharp reversal from centuries of unthinking pronatalism was, of course, caused by the massive demographic changes of the postwar era—changes that have implications reaching far into the future and that do indeed warrant government reactions. Basically, death rates in the developing countries of Asia, Africa, and Latin America, which had been above 30 per thousand between 1900 and 1950, fell to below 20 in the 1960s, while birthrates remained the same or declined very slowly.[1] As a result (see Table 1) annual population growth rates in Asia, for example, doubled from less than 1 percent before 1950 to 2 percent or more by the 1960s; population growth in Africa increased from about 1 percent before 1950 to more than 2 percent thereafter; and population growth in Latin America, already high, increased from about 1.5 percent to nearly 3 percent.

The measures that produced this demographic revolution were primarily control of epidemic diseases such as smallpox and malaria, better food distribution, and nationally oriented development policies assisted by advanced technology from the developed countries. Never called population policy, these programs were categorized, justified, and supported on grounds of health and general development. Nevertheless, their population impact was vast and unprecedented in demographic history. They produced a decline in mortality that was about 10 times as rapid as the one that began in the United States and Europe two centuries ago. In other words, the mortality side of the demographic

[1]UN, Department of Economic and Social Affairs, *The Determinants and Consequences of Population Trends*, New York, 1973 (ST/SOA/Ser. A50), vol. 1, pp. 3–32.

TABLE 1
Estimated Average Annual Percentage Rates of Population Growth for Major Regions, 1900–1950 and 1950–1965

	1900–1950	*1950–1965*
Africa	1.0	2.2
Asia	0.8	2.0
Latin America	1.6	2.8
North America	1.4	1.7
Europe (excluding U.S.S.R.)	0.6	0.8
World	0.8	1.9

SOURCE: UN, Department of Economics and Social Affairs, *Determinants and Consequences of Population Trends*, New York, 1973 (ST/SOA/Ser. A/50), vol. 1, p. 32.

transition in the developing countries compressed into about 20 years the reductions in mortality that had taken 200 years in the now-developed countries.

At the same time, the developed, industrialized countries experienced a much smaller but not negligible postwar population increase beginning in the late 1940s. This was not caused by lower death rates, as in the developing countries, but by a period of higher birthrates. In the United States and Canada, where the boom was most prolonged, the birthrate remained above 20 per thousand until the late 1960s, providing an overall rate of natural increase in North America of more than 1.5 percent throughout the 1950s, or more than double the rate of the 1930s. This contributed to heightened United States awareness of population growth that was translated first into careful academic research and second into growing political concern.

Throughout the 1960s, data documenting phenomenal increases in total world population—2 billion in 1930 to 3 billion in 1960 to 4 billion in the mid-1970s—continued to accumulate.

They were publicized, analyzed, and discussed. A pattern of striking demographic contrasts emerged. Basically, the developed countries averaged birthrates of around 20 per thousand, death rates of around 10, and annual population growth rates of about 1 percent. The developing countries, on the other hand, averaged birthrates above 40, death rates below 20, and annual population growth rates between 2 and 3 percent. A population increasing at 2.5 percent annually doubles every 28 years or is multiplied more than 12 times within a single century. Thus the future prospects for the developing countries, which could barely feed, house, or employ their populations even in the 1960s, were alarming.

Moreover, the strains of population distribution became increasingly apparent. Between 1950 and 1975 the number of people living in urban areas of the developing world tripled, from 258 million to 775 million; the percentage living in urban areas nearly doubled, from 15.7 to 27.3 percent.[2] In South Asia and Latin America the largest growth rates occurred in the largest cities, which had populations of one-half million or more. As a result, the number of people living in these cities has nearly doubled in each decade since 1950. Moreover, since existing city housing has been hopelessly inadequate for the newcomers, the upsurge in migration has produced huge shantytowns and squatter settlements. In some metropolitan areas these settlements account for a third to a half or more of the total population. In Latin America they are growing as much as 12 to 15 percent annually—in other words, doubling in less than 10 years. By this mobility, the great population increase of the past two decades has become more visible and put greater demands on municipal services than a geographically stationary, rural population.

These realities of demographic growth and distribution have been the basic cause of the population-policy revolution.

[2]UN, Department of Economic and Social Affairs, "Selected World Demographic Indicators by Countries, 1950–2000," New York, May 28, 1975 (ESA/P/WP55), p. 3; UN, Department of Economic and Social Affairs, "Growth of the World's Urban and Rural Population, 1920–2000," *Population Studies*, no. 44, New York, 1969, pp. 7–18.

HOW POPULATION POLICIES CHANGED

In addition to these demographic facts, other postwar changes also prompted policies that were less automatically pronatalist. One change was certainly the growth in overall government responsibility. After the Second World War, the emphasis of the communist and socialist governments on economic planning, the determination of the industrialized Western governments to maintain full employment and avoid another depression, and the ambitions of the newly independent states to meet their citizens' basic needs all led to increased government activism. By the 1960s many governments were willing, as they would not have been before, to consider population growth and even fertility control as legitimate fields for national policy. When in 1959 President Eisenhower declared, "I cannot imagine anything more emphatically a subject that is not a proper political or governmental activity or function or responsibility,"[3] he was speaking for an era that had already closed.

The postwar revolution in population policies actually began in 1946 in Japan, where a rapidly growing population found itself suddenly confined to its own island boundaries. Although Americans had often attributed Japan's prewar economic and military expansionism to the pressures of population growth within the country, ironically after the war the United States military government, because of Catholic opposition, denied Margaret Sanger permission to visit Japan and encourage birth control. Nevertheless, the Japanese government, press, and people were well aware of the high rate of Japanese population growth, and it became a topic of national debate. In 1948 the Japanese Diet revised the 1940 Eugenics Protection Law to allow induced abortion for health reasons. Amended again in 1949 and 1952, these revisions legalized sterilization and other forms of contraception and facilitated access to abortion on economic as well as health grounds. Although there was no government-funded family-planning program, the Japanese people responded rapidly to their newly perceived need and to the ready availability of

[3]*New York Times*, December 3, 1959, pp. 1, 18.

89

abortion and other methods of birth control. In a single decade birthrates fell from 34 to 18 per thousand. Because of the central role of abortion, however, other governments, including that of the United States, made no comment. Demographers noted the rapid decline with surprise, but on the whole Japan was regarded as a unique case, relevant neither for the developed Christian nations of the West nor for the less developed nations elsewhere.

Therefore, it was not Japan but rather the major less developed countries of Asia—China, India, and Pakistan—with the largest populations in the world plus high population densities and rapid population growth, which were the first to recognize publicly and officially that the population issue warranted large-scale government intervention. India initiated a government-supported program to provide family-planning supplies and services directly to fertile couples in 1952, and Pakistan did likewise in 1960. The People's Republic of China began and then wavered in its support of a program in the 1950s, but in the late 1960s it embarked on the most intensive combination of propaganda, services, and near-coercive policies in the world.

Despite opposition from the Catholic Church and, to a lesser extent, from traditionalist religious sects elsewhere, by 1975 some 63 developing countries, including 22 in Asia, 21 in Latin America, and 20 in Africa, had initiated family-planning programs (See Table 2, pp. 102–108). Of these, 34 countries containing more than three-quarters of the developing world's population adopted policies explicitly designed to reduce population growth by reducing fertility, whereas 29 countries justified their policies entirely on health grounds.[4] Thus, by 1975, 92 percent of the developing world's population lived under governments that offered some type of support for birth control, including even countries, such as Brazil, which still officially seek a larger population.

Moreover, within the same time period at least 21 developed countries, including the United States, Britain, Germany, Japan, Sweden, Norway, Denmark, the Netherlands, and Canada, had

[4]Dorothy Nortman, "Population and Family Planning Programs: A Factbook," *Reports on Population/Family Planning*, no. 2, 7th ed., Population Council, New York, October 1975, pp. 19–31.

provided some type of national or international assistance for these efforts.[5] These same developed countries had increasingly removed their own internal barriers against the spread of information and services to help individuals control fertility. In fact, by 1975 the United States and most northern European governments were offering subsidized services to low-income groups so that they would enjoy access to family planning on the same basis as access to any other health or social service.

Today only about a dozen countries—Hungary, Romania, Argentina, Burma, Saudi Arabia, and several small Arab and African states—have explicitly pronatalist policies that actively discourage the practice of family planning. Their reasons range from concern over a near-negative rate of growth, as in Eastern Europe, to political and religious conservatism about sexual mores, to concerns about national power vis-à-vis more populous neighbors, as in Saudi Arabia.

The policy process by which governments came to adopt specific measures to reduce fertility has varied from country to country, but the basic pattern is the same. In most countries private voluntary organizations led the way, demonstrating the acceptability of modern contraceptive methods; academically trained experts pronounced the facts; and government civil servants developed the organizational structure. In every country national elites took the lead in pointing to the problem and then in trying to reconcile rational modern policies with opposition from traditionalist religious and communal leaders. As in the determination of national defense or domestic social policies, several different questions or issues concerning population policies had to be favorably resolved in the 1960s before governments could embark on explicit programs to reduce population growth. First, a new policy or tactic had to be recognized as relevant to basic government objectives or strategies; second, it had to be feasible, both technically and politically; third, it had to have some measure of balance or priority in relation to other programs competing for government attention; and fourth, it had

[5]UN, Fund for Population Activities, *1975 Annual Report*, Appendix A: "Government Pledges and Payments, 1967–1975," New York, 1975, pp. 56–57.

to be urgent enough that the costs of postponing implementation would exceed those of immediate action.

Accordingly, in all the developing countries that have so far adopted population policies, the new programs are viewed as relevant to the basic national objectives of economic and social development. The economic rationale as articulated by Coale and Hoover is that lower rates of population growth will mean higher rates of increase in per capita income, higher levels of saving and investment, and a lower ratio of dependent young children as compared with productive workers.[6] In those Asian countries where large populations and high population densities already existed, governments were first to recognize that they could not also afford high rates of population increase. But the same economic rationale was much less convincing to Latin American and African leaders in the early 1960s since many of their countries had small populations and relatively low population densities, even though their rates of population increase were high. In these cases family-planning programs were justified, often with strong international encouragement and support, as a health measure, that is, as a social rather than a strictly economic or income-producing approach to development (unquestionably, high infant and maternal mortality could be sharply reduced by fewer births, widely spaced). Because social change has a lower priority for most governments than economic gain, these countries accorded family planning less attention and still have less active programs.

The technical feasibility of reducing fertility by national programs was also an issue in policy formulation. During the 1950s, when only condoms, diaphragms, and abstinence were recognized means of reducing births, national programs to reach illiterate villagers hardly seemed practical. The new contraceptive technologies of the 1960s—especially the pill and the intrauterine device (IUD)—made national family-planning programs for the first time technically feasible, although still administratively dif-

[6]Ansley Coale and Edgar M. Hoover, *Population Growth and Economic Development in Low Income Countries: A Case Study of India's Prospects*, Princeton University Press, Princeton, N.J., 1958, pp. 18–25.

ficult. Such programs became more feasible politically when significant numbers of the Catholic laity began to use oral contraceptives—encouraged by the research of distinguished Catholic physicians, who argued that the pill did not impose an artificial barrier between egg and sperm, but functioned naturally by creating a hormonal balance similar to pregnancy in which ovulation did not occur.[7] This lay revolt against the proscriptions of the Vatican—buttressed by health and humanitarian arguments as well as the doctrinal argument—greatly weakened the voice of Catholic opposition, although economic arguments probably carried greater weight in high government circles.

The priority that government leaders were first prepared to give fertility-reduction programs depended on their perception of how relevant these programs really were for economic development; how effective they would be in relation to other more visible forms of development such as roads, factories, and schools; and how much of a political hazard they might be. Actually, family-planning programs on a voluntary basis have so far not proved a serious political liability in any country. On the other hand, the fact that family planning is not viewed as a political "vote getter" means that other programs tend to have priority, especially around election time.

The relative lack of urgency with which some governments supported population policies in the 1960s reflected some discounting of future benefits against present costs. Since the real political and economic impact of new births is not felt for 15 to 20 years, it is hardly surprising that many of the new nations with somewhat insecure governments were at first content to leave these programs entirely in the hands of private organizations.

But the pace of population policies, once announced or initiated within a country, has clearly been accelerated by two external factors. One of these is rapidly changing technology, which, sometimes to the embarrassment of political leaders, has surely influenced national programs and demographic change. Simple equipment and improved techniques for pregnancy ter-

[7]John Rock, *The Time Has Come: A Catholic Doctor's Proposals to End the Battle over Birth Control*, Alfred A. Knopf, New York, 1963, pp. 159–178.

mination, for example, have made abortion safer than childbirth. Similarly, new techniques for outpatient female sterilization have brought this procedure out of hospitals or postpartum centers and into clinics and even mobile units and camps. Both abortion and sterilization are methods frequently chosen by women in very different cultures when they are available. Thus, ironically, technological change has made the two methods that are politically the most controversial now technically the safest and the most cost-effective: abortion, as a backup for contraceptive ignorance or failure, and sterilization, as a one-time, trouble-free method for couples who have already had all the children they want. Since 1969, 10 countries (Tunisia, Taiwan, South Korea, Zambia, the United States, India, France, Cyprus, Singapore, and Iran), have removed major restrictions against abortion, making a total of 27 countries with populations over 3 billion that permit relatively easy access to abortion. In the same period, nine countries (Austria, Denmark, Iran, the Philippines, Tunisia, Chile, El Salvador, Pakistan, and Singapore) approved specific policies permitting or encouraging voluntary contraceptive sterilization.[8] Most countries have never actually prohibited sterilization, but ambiguities in older laws, which may, for instance, include sterilization as an "act of mutilation," have made physicians cautious. An administrative requirement for spousal or parental consent is sometimes written into the new programs.

Another external influence on national policy has been the attention that international bodies have focused on population issues. Although the UN and other intergovernmental bodies constantly pay homage to the sovereign rights of all nations to determine their own policies, the fact remains that these agencies are more than merely the sum of their individual government members. International agencies and global issues assume a momentum of their own that, for better or worse, encourages

[8]Relaxed abortion restrictions: Emily Campbell Moore-Cavar, *International Inventory of Information on Induced Abortion*, Columbia University Press for the International Institute for the Study of Human Reproduction, New York, 1974, pp. 76–88. Sterilization policies: Association for Voluntary Sterilization, "Sterilizations performed by IPPF in Asia, 1973–1975," *International Project Newsletter*, New York, 1975, pp. 2–3.

actions that even sovereign governments might not have taken without such pressure.

In the field of population, the UN has for several decades played a prominent role. First, performing a research and data-gathering task, the UN Population Division compiled and published worldwide data on mortality changes and population growth. Then, adding analysis and interpretation, the Division provided an articulate warning of demographic problems and imbalances. Later, in the mid-1960s, when money and trained people were needed to implement some of the projects proposed by the experts, a development assistance role was established through the UN Fund for Population Activities (UNFPA). The UNFPA was at first only a funding mechanism for programs that other UN agencies or recipient countries wanted to undertake; contributions were (and are) voluntary, not assessed. Nevertheless, as its resources have grown to $100 million annually, the UNFPA has become a focus for international consideration of population issues, a source of guidelines and priorities, and an important influence on funding and project policies of governments throughout the world.

Beyond data gathering, publicity, and technical assistance on request, international agencies have moved indirectly toward considering international demographic targets. In the strategy for the Second Development Decade, for example, goals were set for per capita income gains (of 3.5 percent) that in fact required a reduction in annual population growth rates in developing countries to 2.5 percent, a figure that was never explicitly acknowledged as a target.

In an even more discreet manner, the World Bank has tried to take into account success in reducing rapid population growth rates as one among many elements of economic and social progress that indicate creditworthiness. But so far, efforts to set or implement international demographic goals have been fraught with political difficulties. As the actions taken at the Bucharest World Population Conference demonstrated, governments that readily accepted such international health targets as an average life expectancy of 62 years by 1985 and an infant mortality rate in the least developed countries of less than 120 per thousand live births were still reluctant to set a global population growth target such as reaching all eligible couples with family-planning services by 1985. Thus the role of international agencies to date has been one of informing and facilitating national action, but where these agencies have attempted to generate any form of overt global standards or pressure on national policies, they have been rebuffed.

TWO

Population Policy Issues

THE CONTROVERSIES OF BUCHAREST

The Bucharest World Population Conference in August 1974 provided a unique opportunity to put the population issue into broader political perspective. Scheduled at a time when the advocates of family planning per se could not yet document whether this approach would really work (see pp. 125–130) and, even more important, at a time when the developing nations were insistently demanding a complete restructuring of international economic relations, the conference at first seemed to polarize the issue between the Western nations, which gave high priority to reducing population growth, and the developing nations, which gave much higher priority to reducing poverty and global maldistribution of wealth. In the debates, the World Population Plan of Action originally drafted by demographers was revised by political leaders to reflect the demands of the developing world for a new international economic order.[9]

Reacting to the capitalist background and Malthusian basis of Anglo-Saxon thinking, which tended to see overpopulation itself as the cause of poverty, virtually all the developing countries

[9]W. Parker Mauldin et al., "A Report on Bucharest," *Studies in Family Planning*, vol. 5, no. 12, Population Council, New York, December 1975, pp. 357–395; Phyllis T. Piotrow, "World Plan of Action and Health Strategy Approved at Population Conferences," *Population Reports*, series E, no. 2, Population Information Program, Washington, D.C., November 1974, pp. E13–E18.

leaned toward the Marxist position that the real cause of poverty was maldistribution of wealth, both among and between countries, and that overpopulation was a symptom rather than a cause of the basic problem. This argument found support among some Western social scientists, who pointed out that family-planning programs did not automatically produce rapid reductions in fertility. They argued that economic and social development—especially more equitable distribution of economic gains among the poorest sector—would be at least as effective in reducing fertility as family-planning programs, if not more so.[10]

This practical and ideological dilemma was to some extent resolved in the final draft of the World Population Plan of Action. The plan affirmed that "all couples and individuals have the basic right to decide freely and responsibly the number and spacing of their children and to have the information, education and means to do so."[11] At the same time, the plan emphasized that measures of social and economic development, especially improved health, education, and status of women, played a substantial role in reducing high fertility and were also important objectives by and of themselves. Thus, in effect, not only were the means for fertility reduction redefined and broadened, but also the goal of fertility reduction was subordinated to more diffuse goals of social and economic development and justice, ranging from reduced infant mortality to elimination of imperialism and racial discrimination. Symbolic perhaps of the shift in emphasis on both points was the statement by Dr. Karan Singh, Indian Minister of Health and Family Planning, whose government had been the first to call for help in reducing population growth:

It will be difficult for many countries to accept family limitation as a goal in itself unless it is clearly linked to a more equitable distribution of world resources. . . . Population policy . . . cannot be effective un-

[10]William Rich, *Smaller Families through Social and Economic Progress*, monograph no. 7, Overseas Development Council, Washington, D.C., 1973.

[11]UN, Center for Economic and Social Information, "World Population Plan of Action," *Action Taken at Bucharest*, New York, 1974, para. 14(f).

less certain concomitant economic policies and social programs succeed in changing the basic determinants of high fertility. It has truly been said that the best contraceptive is development.[12]

In a sense the Bucharest approach must be considered theoretically sound, an affirmation of the broader academic definition that population policy includes not only reducing birthrates but also reducing death rates and changing the socioeconomic characteristics of a population. In a political sense, too, it is entirely understandable for the developing countries to identify their population crises or pathologies not in terms of birth- or death rates but rather in economic terms, in terms of the pervasive poverty in which their people live. From their point of view, it is this poverty that existed even before the present population growth, not the number of births and deaths, which creates the great imbalance within and between countries.

From a rhetorical point of view, certainly the Bucharest conference placed population issues directly in the context of development. In the UN jargon of the World Population Plan of Action:

Policies whose aim is to affect population trends must not be considered substitutes for socioeconomic development policies but as being integrated with those policies in order to facilitate the solution of certain problems facing both developing and developed countries and to promote a more balanced and rational development.[13]

A key word in the Bucharest compromise was "integration"— on the theoretical level integrating population concerns with broader social and economic planning, and on the programmatic level integrating family-planning services with other social services. In practice, however, this compromise has really produced two separate kinds of implementation. On the one hand, family-

[12]Karan Singh, "Statement, World Population Conference, Bucharest, Aug. 19–30, 1974," *Journal of Family Welfare*, vol. 21, no. 21, September 1974, pp. 3–6.
[13]UN, "World Population Plan of Action," para. 2.

planning and contraceptive distribution projects are being linked with many other service and distribution networks, including those of government field workers, household deliveries, commercial entrepreneurs, local leaders, agricultural extension workers, religious evangelists, schoolteachers, village women's groups, and the like. This community-based, sometimes even community-initiated, approach is becoming a major component of programs to check population growth.

At the same time, those social and economic measures that can indirectly moderate fertility while simultaneously contributing to economic growth and higher standards of living are now also recognized as a legitimate, if somewhat imprecise, element of population policy. These indirect fertility-reducing measures may include reducing infant and child mortality, stimulating the participation of women in development, promoting land and social reform, extending education, ending child labor, and raising the age of marriage. Although these interrelationships have not been fully proven, the very need to analyze them is important. This becomes the task of planning commissions and development economists. Because their conclusions usually carry greater weight in developing-country governments than the pleas of family-planning administrators, who struggle to carry out unlimited service programs with limited resources, this approach may ultimately, if not immediately, reinforce fertility-reduction efforts.

A third element in the population problem was noted at Bucharest, was discussed much more fully at the Habitat Conference on Human Settlements in Vancouver in 1976, and looms larger still today as a critical new component of population policy. This is rapid urbanization and much increased national and international migration. Population distribution, especially maldistribution, is largely a result of rapid population growth, but the policies and programs to deal with it are very different.

Thus population policy, as it has now evolved, runs the gamut from specific measures to reduce fertility to a broader range of indirect policies to population-distribution policies that, from a different angle, touch on some of the fundamental economic strategies of a nation.

FAMILY-PLANNING POLICIES

As Table 2 shows, government support for family-planning services, usually integrated with existing maternal and child health services, is common throughout the world. In most developing countries, however, family-planning services and supplies are actually not available outside urban areas except through the use of field workers, paramedical personnel, and, most recently, community distribution efforts. Thus the next step beyond provision of health-based services is support of extensive nonphysician or community-based distribution programs. These are now a significant factor in the policies and programs of about 30 developing countries. Virtually all governments that have specific demographic goals have moved beyond a physician-based health structure and are using groups such as the Mothers' Clubs in Korea, village mayors' wives in Indonesia, shopkeepers in India and Pakistan, and traditional healers or midwives not only to talk about family planning but also to distribute both condoms and pills (without prescription). Some governments that support family planning mainly on health grounds, such as Tanzania, have also trained paramedical workers in order to provide a range of health services for their rural populations.[14]

This use of traditional networks to disseminate the new technologies of family planning has been an important development of the 1970s. Where local government or village political structures are strong, as in Indonesia or the People's Republic of China, these units have become an important link in contraceptive distribution and education for smaller families and even sources of pressure to encourage regular contraceptive use. Certainly this type of network, which depends entirely on local

[14]See, for example, Planned Parenthood Federation of Korea, *Family Planning through Nonfamily Planning Organizations*, Seoul, 1975; Phyllis T. Piotrow et al., "Contraceptive Distribution—Taking Supplies to Villages and Households," *Population Reports*, series J, no. 5, Population Information Program, Washington, D.C., July 1975, pp. J69–J88; International Planned Parenthood Federation, *Report to Donors*, London, October 1975, pp. 20–23, 37–40.

TABLE 2
Government Policies in Support of Family-Planning Services and Information

	Government-Supported Program	Fertility-Reduction Goal	Use of Field Workers or Community Distribution	Orals, IUDs, Local Methods	Methods Legal			Information, Education, & Communication			
					Sterilization	Unrestricted Importation	Abortion	National Mass Media Efforts	School Programs	Required Premarital Counseling	Community and Social Pressures
Latin America											
Argentina											
Barbados	Y*	Y	Y	Y				Y	Y		
Bolivia	Y		Y	Y							
Brazil	Y		Y	Y	U						
Chile	Y		Y	Y	U	P			Y		
Colombia	Y	Y	Y	Y		P		P			
Costa Rica	Y		P	Y		P					
Cuba	Y		Y	Y	U		U				
Dominican Rep.	Y	Y	Y	Y	U	Y		Y			
Ecuador	Y		Y	Y	Y	P					
El Salvador	Y	Y	Y	Y	Y	P					
Guatemala	Y	Y	Y	Y	Y	P					

	1	2	3	4	5	6	7	8
Haiti	Y		Y	U	P			
Honduras	Y		Y	U	Y			
Jamaica	Y	Y	Y	Y	Y		Y	Y
Mexico	Y	Y	Y	U	Y			
Nicaragua	Y		Y	U	U			
Panama	Y		Y	Y	P			
Paraguay	Y		Y	U	P			
Peru	Y		Y	Y	Y			
Puerto Rico	Y	Y	Y	Y	U			
Trinidad & Tobago	Y	Y					Y	
Uruguay	Y	Y	Y	Y				
Venezuela	Y	P	Y	U				
Europe								
Austria	Y		Y	Y	Y	Y		
Belgium	Y		Y	U	Y	P		
Czechoslovakia	Y		Y		Y	P		
Denmark	Y		Y	Y	P	P	Y	
Finland	Y		Y	Y	Y	Y	P	
France	Y		Y	U	P	Y	P	

TABLE 2 (Continued)
Government Policies in Support of Family-Planning Services and Information

	Govern-ment-Sup-ported Program	Fertility-Re-duction Goal	Use of Field Workers or Com-munity Distribution	Methods Legal				Information, Education, & Communication			
				Orals, IUDs, Local Methods	Sterili-zation	Unre-stricted Impor-tation	Abortion	National Mass Media Efforts	School Programs	Required Premarital Counseling	Com-munity and Social Pressures
Germany (Democratic Republic)	Y			Y	U		Y				
Germany (Federal Republic)	Y			Y	Y	Y					
Hungary	Y			Y	U	U	Y				
Ireland					U						
Italy				Y		Y					
Norway	Y			Y	Y	Y					
Portugal	Y			Y		Y					
Spain						U					
Sweden	Y			Y	P	P	Y				
U.S.S.R.	Y			Y	U		Y				

Country								
Yugoslavia	Y					Y		Y
Oceania								
Australia	Y			Y	Y		Y	
New Zealand	Y			Y	U		Y	
Africa								
Algeria	Y			Y	Y			
Benin	Y		U	U	U			
Botswana	Y	Y	P	Y	Y	P		
Egypt	Y	Y	Y	Y	P			
Ethiopia	Y			Y	U	Y		
Gambia	Y			Y	Y			
Ghana	Y	Y	P	Y	Y	P	P	
Kenya	Y	Y		Y	Y		P	
Lesotho	Y			Y	U	Y		
Liberia	Y			Y	Y			
Mali	Y			Y	Y	U	P	
Mauritius	Y	Y	Y	Y	P		P	
Morocco	Y	Y		Y	U	P		
Mozambique	Y			Y	Y			
Nigeria	Y		Y	Y	Y			
Rhodesia	Y			Y	Y			
South Africa	Y			Y	Y	Y		

TABLE 2 (Continued)
Government Policies in Support of Family-Planning Services and Information

	Government-Supported Program	Fertility-Reduction Goal	Use of Field Workers or Community Distribution	Methods Legal				Information, Education, & Communication			
				Orals, IUDs, Local Methods	Sterilization	Unrestricted Importation	Abortion	National Mass Media Efforts	School Programs	Required Premarital Counseling	Community and Social Pressures
Sudan	Y						U				
Tanzania	Y		Y	Y	Y						
Tunisia	Y	Y	Y	Y	Y	Y	Y				
Uganda	Y			Y		P					
Upper Volta				Y	U	Y					
Zaire	Y			Y	U	P					
Zambia				Y	U	Y	Y				
Asia											
Afghanistan	Y			Y	Y	U					
Bangladesh	Y	Y	Y	Y	Y			P			
Burma											
China	Y	Y	Y	Y	Y		Y	Y	Y	Y	
Fiji	Y	Y	Y	Y	Y			Y	Y	Y	Y

	1	2	3	4	5	6	7	8	9	10
Gilbert & *Ellice I.*	Y									
Hong Kong	Y	Y	Y	Y	Y	Y	Y	U	U	
India	Y	Y	Y	Y	Y	Y	Y	Y		
Indonesia	Y	Y		Y	Y	Y	P	P	Y	Y
Iran	Y	Y		Y	Y	Y	P	Y	Y	
Iraq	Y		Y	Y	Y	P	P			
Israel	Y			P	Y	P				
Japan	Y	P	P	Y	Y	Y	P			
South Korea	Y	Y	Y	Y	Y	P	P			
Malaysia	Y	Y	Y	Y	Y	P	P	P		
Nepal	Y	Y	Y	Y	Y	P	P	Y		
Pakistan	Y	Y	Y	Y	Y	Y	Y			
Philippines	Y	Y	Y	Y	Y	P	Y			
Saudi Arabia										
Singapore	Y	Y	Y	Y	Y	Y	Y	P	Y	
Sri Lanka	Y	Y	Y	Y	Y					
Syria	Y	Y	U							
Taiwan	Y	Y	Y	Y	Y	Y	U			
Thailand	Y	Y	Y	Y	Y	Y	P	P		
Turkey	Y	Y	Y	Y	Y	Y	Y			

107

TABLE 2 (Continued)

Government Policies in Support of Family-Planning Services and Information

| | Govern-ment-Sup-ported Program | Fertility-Re-duction Goal | Use of Field Workers or Com-munity Distribution | Methods Legal | | | | Information, Education, & Communication | | | |
				Orals, IUDs, Local Methods	Sterili-zation	Unre-stricted Impor-tation	Abortion	National Mass Media Efforts	School Programs	Required Premarital Counseling	Com-munity and Social Pressures
Vietnam (N)	Y	Y		Y	Y	U	U				
Vietnam (S)	Y	Y		Y	Y	U	U				
North America											
Canada	Y			Y	Y	P					
United States	Y			Y	Y	Y	Y				

SOURCES: The sources for Tables 2 and 3 include documents from the Population Council, the Population Reference Bureau, the International Planned Parenthood Federation, and the UN Fund for Population Activities, as well as the following specific citations: Carolyn Dean, et al., "Eighteen Months of Legal Change," *Population Reports*, series E. no. 1, Population Information Program, Washington, D.C., July 1974; Emily Campbell Moore-Cavar, *International Inventory of Information on Induced Abortion*, Columbia University Press for the International Institute for the Study of Human Reproduction, New York, 1974; Dorothy Nortman, "Population and Family Planning Programs: A Factbook," *Reports on Population/Family Planning*, No. 2, 7th ed., Population Council, New York, October 1975; Brenda Vumbaco, "Recent Law and Policy Changes in Fertility Control," *Population Reports*, series E. no. 4, Population Information Program, Washington, D.C., March 1976.

participation, is necessary for reaching the rural areas where 70 percent of developing-country populations live.

Whether or not governments support national family-planning programs, only a few pronatalist states restrict individual use of reversible means of contraception, that is, orals, IUDs, condoms, diaphragms, foams, and locally applied methods. A growing number of developing countries (Antigua, Bangladesh, Chile, Fiji, Jamaica, Pakistan, the Philippines, South Korea, Iran, and Iraq) have specifically authorized distribution of oral contraceptives without a doctor's prescription, even though, in fact, orals are usually available in developing-country pharmacies without prescription at the prevailing commercial price. Even those governments that legally retain a prescription requirement for orals or permit only physicians to perform IUD insertions (or abortions) are actually allowing pharmacists, black marketeers, and native midwives to increase their activities.[15]

Developing countries still import most of their contraceptive supplies. Oral contraceptives, although often pressed into tablet form locally, are most economically produced in large pharmaceutical plants in the developed countries which have extensive commercial markets; those few developing countries, like Brazil, that do produce their own oral contraceptives find the costs per cycle two to three times higher than costs to government purchasers in the United States or Europe because the market is much smaller. China is one of the few developing countries with its own extensive oral contraceptive manufacturing industry.[16] Ironically—since contraceptives are necessarily imported by most of these countries for their national programs—a few governments continue to charge duty, thus adding to the purchase price and complicating international assistance efforts. This may

[15]Phyllis T. Piotrow and Calvin M. Lee, "Oral Contraceptives—50 Million Users," *Population Reports*, series A, no. 1, Population Information Program, Washington, D.C., April 1974, pp. A1–A26; Carolyn Dean et al., "Eighteen Months of Legal Change," ibid., series E, no. 1, July 1974, pp. E1–E12; Brenda Vumbaco, "Recent Law and Policy Changes in Fertility Control," ibid., series E, no. 4, March 1976, pp. E41–E52.

[16]Carl Djerassi, "Fertility Limitation through Contraceptive Steroids in the People's Republic of China," *Studies in Family Planning*, vol. 5, no. 1, Population Council, New York, January 1974, pp. 13–30.

indicate that, despite public pronouncements, government support of family planning does not extend to the finance ministry. Similar administrative problems of coordination with other ministries have been major bottlenecks in the larger noncommunist Asian countries.

Sterilization is legal in most of Asia but restricted or in an ambiguous status in a number of Latin American and African countries, where it is specifically permitted only on health grounds. Abortion is still prohibited in most Catholic and Muslim countries, even though it is estimated that 30 million to 50 million abortions occur each year and that abortion is probably still the most widely used fertility control method of all.[17]

Almost all governments that support family planning in order to reduce population growth encourage public information programs and approve of education about population issues and reproduction in the school system as a matter of policy. But implementation is fragmentary, since family-planning program directors, usually located in a health ministry, have little authority over the public information or education ministries. Thus private organizations still play a large role in information and education, both in using the mass media and in encouraging material for in-school use. Only in China does the government require specific premarital counseling on family planning.

INCENTIVES AND DISINCENTIVES

Special incentives and disincentives have been a point of dissension among Western population experts ever since the mid-1960s, when India and Pakistan first paid men and women to undergo sterilization. A decade later, India, Pakistan, Bangladesh, and Tunisia are still the only governments that make direct

[17]John Robbins, "Unmet Needs in Family Planning. A Supplementary Background Paper: Estimated Total Cost of Fertility Control," *Planning for the Future*, International Planned Parenthood Federation 21st Anniversary Conference, London, 1973; Christopher Tietze and Marjorie Cooper Murstein, "Induced Abortion: 1975 Factbook," *Reports on Population/Family Planning*, no. 14, Population Council, New York, December 1975, p. 13.

payments to couples who accept family planning—sterilization primarily. These countries emphasize that payments are compensation for time, wages, and travel rather than family-planning incentives (see Table 3).

While some economists argue that incentives will raise the "demand curve" for fertility reduction, public health workers have a deep-seated objection to compensating people for acting in their own best interests. Moreover, payments to very poor people for practicing birth control could be construed as limiting the voluntary nature of their choice. In any case acceptor incentives, if paid at a high enough level to motivate a large proportion of otherwise unwilling couples, would be very expensive. (In the late 1960s, for instance, in East Pakistan, now Bangladesh, vasectomies had to be discontinued because incentive payments had consumed the whole budget.) Moreover, all those motivated couples who did not need an incentive would also have to be compensated. Since even now most government family-planning programs allow less than 20 U.S. cents per capita for family planning, moderate incentive payments of, say, $5 to $10 per acceptor would require major budget increases. Even though it might be proven theoretically that incentive payments to reduce births would be economically beneficial in the long run, the short-run costs would probably be prohibitive for government programs.

Only if international donors provide the funds needed are incentive programs likely to be undertaken. However, the United States, the largest donor of population assistance, specifically enacted into law in 1977 a previous administrative prohibition on the payment of any incentives.

A more promising way to use incentives may be on a limited scale by businesses, agricultural estates, or other employer groups who can count an immediate gain if trained female workers do not take maternity leave or if family allowances can be limited. In parts of India and Sri Lanka, for example, experiments are under way with incentive payments, retirement bonds, educational benefits, and special credit terms among different groups, but whatever their local success it will probably be fiscally and administratively impossible to translate them into na-

TABLE 3

Government Priority and Use of Incentives, Disincentives, and Coercion in Fertility Control Programs in Countries with Explicit Demographic Objectives

	Government Priority			Incentives						Disincentives					Coercion
	Statements by Gov't. Leaders	Budget over 10¢ Per Capita	Coordination of Population & Development	Services Free of Charge	Adopter Incentives	Retirement Benefits	Educational Benefits for Children	Extended Credit, Reduced Interest	Reduced Child Allowances	Lower Educational Benefits	Reduced Housing Benefits	Reduced Maternity Benefits	Limited Rations	Threat of Job Loss	Fines or Imprisonment [1]
Africa															
Botswana															
Egypt	Y*		Y												
Ghana		Y	Y	P											
Kenya		Y													
Mauritius		Y	Y	Y											
Morocco					Y										
Tunisia	Y	Y	Y	Y	Y										
Asia															
Bangladesh	Y		Y	Y	Y										
China	Y	Y	Y	Y					Y	Y	Y	Y	P	P	P

112

Fiji	Y			P				
Gilbert & Ellice I.	Y							
Hong Kong		Y						
India		Y	Y	Y	P	Y		
Indonesia		Y	Y	Y				
Iran		Y		Y				
Korea		Y	P	P			Y	
Malaysia		Y		Y				
Nepal		Y						
Pakistan		Y	Y	P	Y		Y	Y
Philippines		Y	Y	Y			Y	Y
Singapore		Y		Y		Y	Y	
Sri Lanka		Y		P	P	Y		
Taiwan		Y		Y		Y		
Thailand	Y							
Turkey			Y					
Latin America								
Barbados								
Colombia		Y	Y					
Costa Rica	Y	Y	Y					

TABLE 3 (Continued)

Government Priority and Use of Incentives, Disincentives, and Coercion in Fertility Control Programs in Countries with Explicit Demographic Objectives

	Government Priority				Incentives					Disincentives				Coercion	
	Statements by Gov't. Leaders	Budget over 10¢ Per Capita	Coordination of Population & Development	Services Free of Charge	Adopter Incentives	Retirement Benefits	Educational Benefits for Children	Extended Credit, Reduced Interest	Reduced Child Allowances	Lower Educational Benefits	Reduced Housing Benefits	Reduced Maternity Benefits	Limited Rations	Threat of Job Loss	Fines or Imprisonment
Dominican Rep.		Y													
El Salvador			Y	Y											
Guatemala			Y												
Jamaica		Y													
Mexico		Y													
Trinidad & Tobago															
Venezuela		Y													

*Y = yes, P = partial.

SOURCE: See source note for Table 2.

tionwide programs. Community incentives to villages or provinces that meet certain targets, for example, have been proposed in India and Bangladesh but have not been implemented.[18]

In contrast to incentives, which are politically popular but financially costly, disincentives add no immediate economic costs to the government budget but entail a high political cost. In fact, in any form of popular government, explicit disincentives may be politically viable only if most of the population is already convinced of the need for restraint. Then, as in Singapore, such policies may reinforce long-term trends. So far, disincentives such as restricted access to public housing, reduced maternity benefits, or limited educational opportunities after the birth of the third child have been implemented only in Singapore *after* birthrates initially fell and in the People's Republic of China *after* the government established firm political control in the late 1960s.

Moreover, from an ethical point of view, both incentives and disincentives have the effect of penalizing the innocent third or fourth child or the large family that needs help most. The sins of the parents are truly visited upon the children if any of the family is deprived of higher income, better housing, or educational help because of additional births. In aggregate terms, such policies could only be described as regressive, benefitting smaller families, which usually have higher per capita incomes, at the cost of larger families with lower per capita incomes.

India has experimented with coercive programs, and two Indian states, Maharashtra and the Punjab, were the first to attempt to pass laws authorizing fines or imprisonment for couples who refused sterilization or some other form of birth control after the second child. In fact, in what could be regarded only as a sharp reversal of his government's policy at Bucharest, Dr. Singh announced in April 1976:

It is clear that simply to wait for education and economic development to bring about a drop in fertility is not a practical solution. The very

[18]Oliver D. Finnigan, *Incentive Approaches in Population Planning Programs*, Office of Health and Public Services, U.S. Agency for International Development, Manila, 1972; Edward Pohlmann, *Incentives and Compensations in Birth Planning*, monograph 2, Carolina Population Center, Chapel Hill, N.C. 1971.

increase in population makes economic development slow and more difficult of achievement. The time factor is so pressing, and the population growth so formidable, that we have to get out of the vicious circle through a direct assault upon this problem as a national commitment.[19]

Thus, despite previous rhetoric, India seemed to be asserting not that development was the best contraceptive, but rather that contraception was a prerequisite to development.

In any case, India's coercive efforts backfired. Muslim villagers protested efforts of local officials to round up a target number for sterilization. Opposition to male sterilization particularly became an important element in the political opposition to Indira Gandhi's authoritarian rule, and for the first time the Congress party was defeated. It will be unfortunate indeed if the government's resort to coercive policies has slowed the progress of voluntary family-planning programs, particularly sterilization, throughout South Asia.

POLICIES INDIRECTLY AFFECTING FERTILITY

The Bucharest World Population Conference, as noted previously, put special emphasis on the interrelationship of population policies and development and urged that "countries wishing to affect fertility levels give priority to implementing development programmes and educational and health strategies which, while contributing to economic growth and higher standards of living, have a decisive impact upon demographic trends, including fertility."[20]

Unfortunately, social science research has not yet conclusively demonstrated what policies these might be nor with what rapidity or cost-effectiveness they might produce this result. There is a high correlation between level of education, employment, higher status of women, and delayed age of marriage, on the one hand,

[19]Karan Singh, "National Population Policy," mimeo., New Delhi, April 16, 1976, p. 1.
[20]UN, "World Population Plan of Action," para. 31.

and low fertility on the other. There is much less conclusive evidence that improved health, lower infant mortality, prohibition of child labor, systems to provide compulsory education, increased urbanization, some means of providing for old-age security, more equitable distribution of income, rural development, and land reform may also eventually lead to lower fertility.[21] And there is the still-unproved ex post facto argument that development alone produces lower birthrates. This argument is based largely on the fact that all the now-developed countries have birthrates below 20 per thousand and that birthrates have declined fastest in countries that have experienced most rapid development: Japan, Korea, Taiwan, Hong Kong, and Singapore. On the other hand, there is new evidence from studies of the demographic transition in Europe that innovations such as family planning spread through regional patterns, as the idea becomes acceptable, as its advantages are recognized, and as effective techniques become available.[22] These conditions occur in modern or developed societies, but they can also be made to occur in less modernized communities, and they can be stimulated by efforts of national and community leaders.

To date, raising the age of marriage, which has a strong and direct influence on fertility and requires no government expenditure, has been the social policy most widely used for the purpose of reducing fertility. Since 1970, 11 developing countries (Bangladesh, China, Colombia, Cuba, India, Indonesia, Iran, Malaysia, Nepal, Tanzania, and Tunisia) have raised the legal age of marriage for women and usually for men as well.[23] But these laws are difficult to enforce, and with the noteworthy exception of

[21]William P. McGreevey, *The Policy Relevance of Recent Social Research on Fertility*, Occasional Monograph series no. 2, Interdisciplinary Communications Program, Smithsonian Institution, Washington, D.C., September 1974, pp. 1–59.

[22]Ansley Coale, "The Demographic Transition Reconsidered," *International Population Conference, Liège 1973*, International Union for the Scientific Study of Population, Liège, Belgium, 1974, vol. 1, p. 69.

[23]Rebecca Cook and Katherine Piepmeier, "Equity under the Law," *World Health*, World Health Organization, Geneva, August—September 1976, pp. 4–9.

China, most countries set a lower limit below age 20—still young enough to permit many pregnancies.

Most of the developing countries are moving to adopt some of the other policies listed, but not primarily for reasons of fertility control. Since most of these measures, including those that affect women, require some reallocation of political or economic power within the country, they can be implemented only slowly. Even the passage of laws eliminating child labor or discrimination against women, for instance, is often more symbolic than real.

Implementation, of course, depends partly on the priority accorded an issue within the government. The most obvious measures of policy priority for fertility reduction are high levels of government expenditure and public support from the head of state. Table 3 shows a mixed picture. On the positive side, governments with demographic, as opposed to health, objectives rank high on both counts. However, despite the post-Bucharest efforts to integrate fertility-reduction programs with overall development planning, few governments have the trained personnel or organizational capacity to coordinate population and development policies, evaluate the impact of other policies on fertility, or undertake extensive demographic or fertility-related research, even though such research might be useful in identifying indigenous approaches or adaptations of Western technology.

POPULATION DISTRIBUTION POLICIES

Policies on population distribution are more difficult to define and implement than specific fertility control policies. Nevertheless, as of the mid-1970s they have been increasingly recognized as an important element of national population policy. A UN survey of 98 developing countries taken at the time of the Bucharest conference revealed that 49 of them considered present levels of metropolitan growth excessive and 55 were implementing some type of policy to divert migrants from metropolitan regions.[24]

[24]UN Population Conference, June 20, 1974, "Population Policies and Programmes," mimeo., (E/CONF60/CBP/21), tables 17 and 19.

It has been reasonably well established that in the past most migrants, being a self-selected group, were male (except in Latin America); they were between the ages of 15 and 30, unmarried, better educated than nonmigrants, more venturesome, influenced by expectations of economic gain, and more likely to move to cities where relatives or friends had preceded them. It has also been shown that, despite the hardships they encounter, the majority of migrants have high expectations and do not want to return.[25] As individuals, they may benefit from moving to the cities, but the social impact on the communities where they settle has, like the impact of high fertility, been disturbing enough to governments to precipitate more active population policies to influence and moderate this flow of migration.

In the past, opinion has been divided, both among academic experts and national planners, as to the advantages and disadvantages of migration to urban areas. Traditionally cities have been seen as vital forces for modernization, as "the essential and successful centers and transmission belts of the new technological system."[26] Economists have tended to stress the economic gain of urbanization to individual migrants and to the economy as a whole. Sociologists, on the other hand, have pointed to the loss of community roots and lack of productive work. They see the new migrants as human flotsam and jetsam that has been uprooted from traditional agriculture without being incorporated into modern industry. Political scientists are also beginning to note the growing feelings of political impotence and of alienation from local government activities even in developed countries.[27]   Moreover, even though the majority of migrants

[25]Michael P. Todaro, *Internal Migration in Developing Countries*, International Labor Organization, Geneva, 1976, pp. 65–66; Ghazi Farooq, "Population Distribution and Migration," in Warren Robinson (ed.), *Population and Development Planning*, Population Council, New York, 1975, pp. 134–152.

[26]Barbara Ward, "The Cities That Came Too Soon," *The Economist*, December 6, 1969, pp. 56–62.

[27]Cf. Harley L. Browning, "Migrant Selectivity and the Growth of Large Cities in Developing Societies," *Rapid Population Growth*, vol. 2, Johns Hopkins University Press for the National Academy of Sciences, Baltimore, 1971, pp. 273–274; Daniel Lerner, "Comparative Analysis of Processes of Modernization," in Horace Miner (ed.), *The City in Modern Africa*, Praeger Publishers,

may have improved their individual positions, their presence in the cities has put a heavy burden on municipal budgets. Basic city services, such as roads, potable water, sewerage systems, electricity, transportation, schools, and health facilities, are expensive, and the migrants themselves cannot pay the taxes to provide them. The problems of impoverished cities have quickly become the financial problems of national governments, and that is why governments are now being forced to formulate explicit policies influencing population distribution or migration. These immigration, ruralization, urbanization, or regional development policies, as they may also be called, are being formulated for much the same reason that governments formulated fertility control policies. Uncontrolled migration, like uncontrolled fertility, impedes other development objectives. Therefore, policies to deal with it have become relevant and urgent in relation to overall government priorities, and virtually all developing countries are now experimenting with a number of different approaches.

At present, five different patterns of population-distribution policy can be identified, though they often exist simultaneously in the same country or even the same region. They are (1) rapid urbanization, (2) modernization of agriculture, (3) integrated rural development, (4) dispersed urbanization, and (5) regional development.[28]

The first two—rapid urbanization and agricultural modernization—have not been so much deliberate government population policies as the incidental result of other economic measures, such as location of the factories and industrial jobs (paying minimum wages) in urban areas, the implementation of cheap-food policies in these areas, or the introduction of heavy equipment and capital-intensive farming techniques in overcrowded rural areas. These policies, combined with the enormous population increases caused by disease eradication programs, have had a

---

Inc., New York, 1967, pp. 21–38; Sharon Camp, "Modernization: Threat to Community Politics," Ph.D. dissertation, Johns Hopkins University, Baltimore, October 1976.

[28] Sally Evans Findley, "Planning for International Migration: A Review of the Issues and Policies," chap. 5 and summary, paper for GE-Tempo Center for Advanced Studies, Washington, D.C., September 12, 1976.

massive and irreversible impact on population distribution that was not fully intended or foreseen. Together they created the pull of the urban centers, toward jobs that unfortunately did not exist in adequate numbers for all those who sought them, and the push of the rural areas, where tractors, electric pumps, and the need for heavy investment in fertilizers, irrigation, and improved seeds drove an ever-increasing number of poor farmers off the land.

The other strategies—integrated rural development, dispersed urbanization, and regional development—are explicit population-distribution programs deliberately designed to counteract the adverse effects of excessively rapid urbanization and rural impoverishment. Many developing countries are just beginning to support pilot projects along these lines. Integrated rural development means primarily efforts to provide health services, education, agricultural extension services, credit, and a broad array of other social and economic services as well as jobs in rural areas. The most successful of these efforts involve a high level of local participation and leadership.

Dispersed-urbanization policies have been adopted to deflect internal migration from the largest or central cities to provincial cities, market towns, or even new centers such as Brasília. Such policies might include selective road building, location of new industry or educational centers, or various employment bonuses. Regional development efforts use similar incentives to attract migrants to unsettled areas or regions with extensive resources to be developed. All these policies are experimental, without a proven record of success even in the developed countries, but more and more nations are trying to guide population movement by such a deliberate planning of economically productive facilities.

Like policies to influence fertility, policies to influence migration or distribution may be voluntary or coercive, may offer positive benefits or withhold benefits for noncompliance. They may be highly centralized or dependent largely on local initiative. At present, most distribution and fertility policies rely on a rational model of human behavior, assuming that people will act in their own best interests without government coercion. But a number of governments, especially the communist states, have gone much further in restricting population movement and jobs than in restricting fertility. Significantly, the most stringent distribution policies, like the most stringent family-planning policies, have been those of the People's Republic of China, implemented under strict totalitarian control, occasionally by coercive measures. Certainly noncoercive methods—that is, broad development programs or specific incentives or disincentives—that do in fact have the desired demographic effect are difficult to devise. As with fertility-influencing programs, incentives that reward people to live in a prescribed location are economically expensive; and disincentives that discourage people from moving are politically hazardous even to totalitarian governments. Thus many of the difficult political as well as moral constraints that have troubled fertility-regulating policies will surely also trouble distribution policies as the pressures of population growth increase. Which, for example, is a greater infringement on the personal freedoms that Americans value: restricting freedom of movement or restricting freedom of reproduction? Is it possible, in a world of rapidly increasing population, not to restrict some elements of freedom?

There are still further difficulties in implementing population-distribution policies. With regard to fertility, for example, many individuals in the developing countries do not want as many children as they have, and thus high fertility rates can be and have been to some extent affected simply by distributing contraceptive supplies and services, that is, by giving individuals a choice. Migration, however, begins as a deliberate act of choice, one that can be influenced only by presenting preferable counterchoices or strong prohibitions. Furthermore, in the fertility field, the developed countries, whatever their other failings, do offer a uniform example of low fertility and a wide array of safe birth control methods that have proved effective for all people, regardless of their level of affluence or education. In the area of population distribution, however, the developed countries offer few good models for solving problems of urban crowding, suburban sprawl, or rural stagnation; moreover, much of the capital-intensive technology of Western industry, related both to urban planning and to agricultural development, is inappropriate and often counterproductive in developing countries, which have a surplus of unskilled labor and a deficit of technical know-how.

Another difference is that population-distribution policies necessarily have international as well as national components, since an increasing number of migrants cross national borders. Although fertility control has important long-term international significance, the fertility issue does not spill over into international policy in quite as literal or immediate a sense as migration.

International migration has the same root cause as national migration: too many people and not enough attractive job opportunities in the home location. Just as landless rural laborers in the developing countries look to the nearest city to improve themselves, so doctors, scientists, managers, and semiskilled workers in the cities of the developing world look to the affluent countries for higher pay and better living conditions.

International migration, however, whether permanent or temporary, whether of skilled or unskilled workers, whether with or without their families, has so far been more effectively controlled by national governments than internal migration. Internal migration policies tend to be characterized by long-term positive objectives that are difficult to achieve, whereas international immigration and emigration policies are usually characterized by specific negative objectives and restrictions on individual freedom that at least some governments can enforce. Every country places some restrictions on migration to or from foreign countries. By contrast, only a handful—the communist countries, South Africa, and Tanzania—seriously restrict internal movement. Ironically, the coercion and forced return that are the normal fate of unwanted international migrants who are caught would be bitterly condemned if applied domestically. Yet these policies are just beginning to be questioned on the international level, even though international migration policies resulting in "white" Australia and the expulsion of Asians from certain African countries have been more blatantly nationalist or racist than almost any other type of population policy.[29] In fact, one

[29]It is noteworthy that the establishment of an "independent" Transkei Republic in South Africa has not been accepted internationally. This move is seen as a subterfuge to apply accepted international migration policies to what might more appropriately be treated as a domestic population-distribution issue.

123

might argue that, unlike internal population policies in most countries, international migration policies have often defied clear economic benefits in order to promote nationalistic or emotional causes.

Actually, population-distribution policies, especially internal-distribution policies, are still in their infancy, perhaps a decade or more behind family-planning policies in the specifics of definition, implementation, and evaluation. Whereas several nations have reached a low fertility and low mortality equilibrium, and the means are at hand for others to do so, the problems of population distribution have remained fairly intractable and may even intensify with each new generation. In fact, present demographic trends suggest that by the 1980s policies to deal with migration and distribution will be more controversial and complex than policies dealing with fertility. The most recent data suggest that population-growth issues will revolve less around fertility rates, which seem now to be declining rapidly around the world, and more around a lopsided age structure among those people already born who will be alive in the 1980s.

THREE

Fertility Trends and Policies

FERTILITY TRENDS IN THE 1980s

The demographic picture for the late 1970s and 1980s is still not entirely clear, in part because most current projections (principally those of the UN) were prepared in 1973 largely on the basis of 1970 population data. These data do not yet reflect the demographic impact of extensive new family-planning programs, most of which moved into high gear only in the early 1970s. Close observers, including the eminent statistician Sir Maurice Kendall, Director of the World Fertility Survey, believe that vital rates may now be changing so rapidly that even the selected sampling of fertility patterns done in 1974 and 1975 by the World Fertility Survey may not fully reflect the extent of the change today. Thus many of the data now widely circulated are no longer reliable guides. For example, the published UN medium variant still assumes that world population growth rates will not begin to decline until the period 1980–1985 (when they are estimated to drop from 1.95 to 1.93 percent annually),[30] although many others believe this turning point occurred between 1970 and 1975.

Analyses in 1976 and 1977 by the U.S. Agency for International Development (USAID), by the Worldwatch Institute, and by the

[30]Sir Maurice Kendall, Chairman, Program Steering Committee of the World Fertility Survey, personal communication, October 29, 1976; UN, Department of Economic and Social Affairs, Population Division; *World Population Prospects as Assessed in 1973.* New York, 1977 (ST/ESA/Ser.A60), p. 14.

125

Population Council all suggest that the UN data are indeed lagging behind events. In January 1976 the Director of the USAID Office of Population concluded that by 1974 the annual population-growth-rate curve had already turned downward from 2 percent in 1965 to 1.63 percent in 1974, and the total annual increment in population had dropped from 66 million to 63 million. In November 1976 a Worldwatch Institute study also suggested that the corner had been turned. As of mid-1975 world population growth had dropped from 1.90 percent to 1.64 percent annually, representing an annual increment of 64 million.[31] Even the UN Population Division noted in its report to the UN Population Commission in January 1977:

So far as the present main indications go, perhaps the outstanding unambiguous fact emerging from the programmes to date concerns the large numbers of persons in higher-fertility areas who have been found willing to adopt, or at least experiment with, birth-limiting behavior patterns. Reproductive propensities in many high-fertility areas, far from being the monolithic or tradition-dominated entities presupposed by conventional theory and simplified description, have been found on closer examination to show considerable flexibility, extensive variability among groups and individuals, and high latent potential for rapid change. Even with a large allowance for misinterpretation or incorrect estimation of the facts, or for recidivism in behaviour by temporary programme participants, it seems clear that many millions residing in numerous parts of the high-fertility regions have been willing to adopt family-limiting methods on both permanent and temporary bases.[32]

The varying worldwide statistics all may suffer somewhat from the "fallacy of misplaced precision," since a large factor in the world population situation is represented by the People's Re-

---

[31]USAID figures: R. T. Ravenholt, "World Population Crisis and Action toward Solution," paper presented at dedication of Prentice Women's Hospital and Maternity Center, Chicago, January 19, 1976, pp. 4, 9; Worldwatch study: Lester Brown, *World Population Trends: Signs of Hope, Signs of Stress*, paper 8, Worldwatch Institute, Washington, D.C., October 1976, p. 7.

[32]UN, Economic and Social Council, Population Commission, "Concise Report on Monitoring of Population Trends," New York, November 8, 1976, (E/CN.9/23), para. 99.

public of China, for which no official figures have been released. R. T. Ravenholt of USAID and Lester Brown of Worldwatch believe that China's birthrate has dropped below 20 per thousand—which would be lower than that of any other developing country—producing an annual population-growth rate of close to 1 percent. If accurate, these figures would represent an unprecedented drop in the birthrate for a large, poor, and underdeveloped country, from 35 per thousand in 1965 to 14 to 19 per thousand in 1975. Still, there are no hard data available to contradict the USAID and Worldwatch figures, and the data reported by visitors to China from specific areas or proferred by high-ranking Chinese government officials confirm low figures.[33]

Even without this speculation on Chinese fertility and on the success of the comprehensive and coercive Chinese family-planning program, however, it is possible to document substantial declines in fertility in other developing countries which were almost certainly the result of explicit fertility control policies. The 1976 Population Council *Reports on Population/Family Planning*, a generally authoritative source, shows that even by 1974 there were declines in birthrates in a dozen of the larger countries of the developing world, as compared with 1970 figures.

During the period 1977–1978 fertility surveys from more than a dozen developing countries sponsored by the International Statistical Institute/World Fertility Survey will be released. Based on 1974–1975 surveys of about 10,000 couples in each country, this will be the most complete, accurate, and up-to-date information available on contraceptive attitudes and practices and resulting fertility in the developing world. With the exception of a few countries, such as Pakistan, these studies are expected to show contraceptive usage increased over earlier surveys and birthrates on an accelerating downward curve.

To what extent are these declines the result of explicit population policies and organized family-planning programs? To

[33]R. T. Ravenholt, "The Chinese Puzzle," *People*, vol. 3, no. 4, 1976, p. 51; Brown, *World Population Trends*, p. 9.; Judith Banister, "Mortality, Fertility, and Contraceptive Use in Shanghai, The People's Republic of China," paper presented at the Annual Meeting of the Population Association of America, Montreal, April 1976, p. 14.

TABLE 4
Declines in Birthrates in Selected Large Developing Countries,
1970–1974

Country	Crude Birthrate 1970*	Crude Birthrate 1974*
India	40–50	36–37
Brazil	41–43	38–40
Philippines	44–50	36†
Thailand	40–45	37
Turkey	40	31–35
Egypt	45	34–36
South Korea	32–34	24–28
Colombia	41–44	30–33
Sri Lanka	32	27.3
Venezuela	46–48	36
Malaysia	37	30
Chile	34–36	23.2
Tunisia	45	36

*Per 1,000.
†1975 data.
SOURCE: Dorothy Nortman, "Population and Family Planning Programs: A Factbook," *Reports on Population/Family Planning*, June 1971 and October 1976.

what extent are they the result of other factors, such as social and economic development, that would have occurred regardless of family-planning efforts? In the specialized field of family-planning evaluation, this is a much-debated issue, somewhat like the medieval question of how many angels could dance on the head of a pin. An overview by Berelson and Freedman in 1975 concluded that "family planning programs make a difference that matters'' and may indeed be more significant than the effect of the social setting.[34]

A detailed study in Colombia suggested that organized family-planning programs and commercial contraceptive programs were responsible for about half of the rapid decline in fertility between 1964 and 1977. The other half was attributed to higher incomes, increased female education, and rapid urbanization—although it is hard to see how these changes in social setting could themselves reduce fertility unless they were translated into either increased continence or higher rates of contraceptive use. In Sri Lanka and several other Asian countries, an increase in the age of marriage is given credit for about half the decline in total fertility, from about 38.7 births per thousand in 1953 to 27.2 in 1975.[35] Age of marriage increases when men and/or women seek higher education, cannot find suitable income-producing employment, or migrate, or when the balance between eligible men and women at appropriate ages is skewed. These factors are influenced by social and economic change. The difficulty of weighing the impact of these as against the impact of an ongoing and well-publicized family-planning program is rather like comparing apples and oranges. Generally speaking, family-planning programs or practices (including abortion) are the direct and immediate cause of fertility declines, but over the longer run socioeconomic factors indirectly influence both the willingness of couples to use family planning and the ability of family-planning information and service providers to reach potential users.

With the important exceptions of India, Pakistan, and Bangladesh, where long-standing and well-publicized programs have been poorly administered, all the developing countries with ex-

---

[34]Ronald Freedman and Bernard Berelson, ''The Record of Family Planning Programs,'' *Studies in Family Planning*, vol. 7, no. 1, Population Council, New York, January 1976, p. 19.

[35]Joseph E. Potter, Myriam Ordonez, and Anthony R. Measham, ''The Rapid Decline in Colombian Fertility,'' *Population and Development Review*, vol. 2, nos. 3 and 4, September–December 1976, pp. 509–528; Siva Chinnatamby, ''Family Planning Helps in Sri Lanka,'' in *Draper World Population Fund Report No. 4*, Spring 1977, Washington, D.C., pp. 23–25.

tensive family-planning programs have experienced rapid fertility declines. Indonesian officials estimate that in the six years between 1970 and 1976 the crude birthrate for Java and Bali, where an extensive village-based family planning program is underway, has fallen from 41 to 33. In Taiwan, the percentage of illiterate women ever using contraception increased from 19 to 78 in 11 years between 1965 and 1976 when organized family planning programs were vigorously underway. Even a country like Mexico, which embarked on a family planning program only in 1973, has already reportedly experienced a decline in population growth from about 3.5 to 3.1 percent in two years. In fact, in reviewing the progress of organized family planning programs in Asia, Professor Ronald Freedman, at the University of Michigan, a widely respected United States demographer, concluded that "the idea and practice of family limitation can sweep an LDC population far more quickly than we had previously imagined possible."[36] Thus the impact of organized family-planning programs is increasingly evident.

At the same time, crude birthrates in the developed world have also continued to fall, even though the number of women in their twenties, the prime reproductive years, has increased (because of the high birthrates in the 1950s). Four countries—East and West Germany, Austria, and Luxembourg—have already reached zero population growth, that is, an equal number of births and deaths annually; and many other European countries, as well as the United States, are close to that point. In the Eastern European countries, which have the lowest birthrates in the world, family planning and abortion have been legal and available for many years. A new trend toward pronatalism has led Hungary and Romania to restrict abortion and provide incentives for larger families. Nevertheless, after an initial rise, their birthrates are

---

[36] Haryono Suyono and Thomas H. Reese, "Integrating Village Family Planning and Primary Health Services: The Indonesian Perspective," *Testimony before the U.S. House of Representatives, Select Committee on Population,* April 27, 1978, p. 13; Ronald Freedman, "Social Science Research on Population in Asia," *Testimony before the U.S. House of Representatives Select Committee on Population,* April 27, 1978, p. 9; *New York Times,* January 9, 1977, p. 11.

still near replacement level and seem highly resistant to government pronatalist pressures.

Thus, in most of the world, evidence now suggests that birthrates are responsive to the messages and methods that family-planning programs disseminate. The issue for policy makers today should not be whether family planning works, but how government programs can bring family planning to those who still do not have access to it—above all, the young, the remote rural villagers, and the lowest income groups—and how family planning can be reinforced or accelerated through other kinds of programs.[37]

FERTILITY CONTROL POLICIES FOR THE 1980s

Even if birthrates continue to fall sharply, world population will continue to grow simply because of the large number of young people already born who will enter their reproductive years in the next two decades. As Tomas Frejka has calculated, even if the whole world reaches an average reproduction rate of two children per couple in the 1970s—which is highly unlikely—world population will increase until the middle of the next century, stabilizing then at a level of nearly 6 billion people.[38]

The number of potential young parents in the 1980s is not open to question. All those who will be age 15 or older by 1990 have already been born. In 1975 there were approximately 1.1 billion children in the developing world below the age of 15—about 40 percent of its total population.[39] If more than 90 percent survive for the next 15 years, then by 1990 there will be about one billion young adults in the developing world aged 15 to 30, or 250 million more than today. These young adults will be in their peak reproductive years.

What kind of population policies will be feasible under these

[37]Bruce Stokes, *Filling the Family Planning Gap*, Paper no. 12, Worldwatch Institute, Washington, D.C., May 1977, pp. 1–8.

[38]Tomas Frejka, *The Future of Population Growth*, John Wiley & Sons, New York, 1973, pp. 51–82.

[39]Calculated from UN, "Selected World Demographic Indicators," p. 3.

demographic conditions? What programs or initiatives should governments support in the 1980s to cope with the needs of this new generation?

The most obvious and appropriate response for governments will be to support and extend voluntary family-planning services so that they are genuinely available to every person of child-bearing age. This new generation will not be shocked or frightened by family planning because they will have heard it discussed all their lives. They will tend to use contraceptives just as they use toothpaste and soft drinks if they are convenient, effective, safe, and satisfactory in meeting personal needs. Thus governments should encourage all local public health facilities as well as commercial channels and a variety of local groups to disseminate information and services. All the present methods—and perhaps a few new ones such as chemical abortifacients, injectables, and immunological methods—should be made widely available after any necessary testing has been done to prove that they are safer than furtive methods for dealing with unwanted pregnancy. Chemical abortifacients such as prostaglandin suppositories and orally active compounds that can induce abortion will probably become available by the early 1980s. Whether formally approved by government regulatory agencies or not, "abortion pills" may be as difficult to restrict in the next decade as narcotics are today.

Governments should discourage the tendency to treat family planning as a medical problem. Physicians will continue to play a role in providing such surgical means as sterilization and abortion, in training other practitioners, and in handling the complications that are inevitable whenever millions of people use any drug or device. But most of the people who want family planning are not sick. Paramedical staff or, in the developing countries, trained indigenous midwives should provide family-planning assistance just as they provide obstetrical attention and all other forms of family health care.

Voluntary sterilization, which has the lowest failure rate of any method and very few complications, will probably become more popular despite the condemnation of the present Pope. Moreover, as infant and child mortality continue to decline, sterilization will appeal to younger couples and, it is hoped, to conscientious fathers as well as weary mothers. Governments should begin now to provide quality sterilization services on a voluntary basis, especially for women, who then tend to become active word-of-mouth promoters of the method. With better insertion techniques and follow-up, IUDs may also become more acceptable. With or without the approval of the U.S. Food and Drug Administration, which has been delayed because of American political constraints, three-month and six-month injectables will spread rapidly throughout the developing countries.

As motivation for smaller families grows and as young people recognize that family size can be controlled, the incidence of abortion will surely rise. Until simple, foolproof contraceptive methods are developed that everyone can tolerate medically and accept psychologically, and until human error is reduced as much as possible, abortion is virtually inevitable, whether fully legalized or not. Moreover, it is likely that improved techniques will permit the termination of pregnancy even earlier than six to eight weeks. As the techniques become simpler, nonphysicians will play an increasingly important role in providing them. In fact, self-administered abortion by chemical means may soon eliminate the need for any intervention by a third party.

Abortion will remain a difficult issue for many governments to deal with because both Catholic and Muslim religious leaders continue to resist legalization. Yet because of the very number of young women who will look on abortion as a necessary resort when other methods fail, it is likely that the traditionalist opposition of older generations will gradually become less potent. In any case, whether governments legalize abortion and make it a safe, acceptable alternative for this hard-pressed generation or whether they continue to leave it in the province of the busy illegal abortionist, there seems little doubt that it will continue to be a major factor in helping individuals control their own fertility.

Adolescent pregnancies will also cause increasing trouble for government policy makers. Illegitimate teen-age pregnancies are already a serious problem in developed countries. Yet politicians and parents both prefer to think, before the event, that out-of-wedlock pregnancy won't happen to their children and, after the event, that it was someone else's fault. Governments or parents can try to reduce teen-age pregnancy by enforcing a puritanical moral climate with strict separation of sexes, by requiring physically exhausting employment to fill all available time, or by providing convenient access to, and sympathetic counseling about, contraceptives. In totalitarian societies like the People's Republic of China, puritanism and hard work are enforced by the state. In less regimented societies, counseling and help with contraceptives—thus expanding rather than restricting present freedoms—may be the only practical way to reduce adolescent pregnancy. In any case, countries with high levels of young-adult unemployment and no strict traditions against sexual activity, especially by young males, are likely to be troubled by high rates of adolescent pregnancy.

Thus, despite conservative religious and parental opposition and with or without full government backing, family-planning programs will have to serve a younger clientele. Similarly, public information, mass media, and educational institutions should devote more attention to the family-planning problems and needs of young people. For example, commercial advertising of contraceptives on radio and television, still prohibited in the United States, should be extended rapidly, especially in countries where radio is the most important way to reach rural youth. Instead of general exhortations to "plan your family," mass media should provide more specific information on existing types of contraceptives, how they are used, and where they are available.

With respect to the organization and administration of family-planning services, great progress should be possible by the 1980s. As the poor countries develop more experience in public administration, they should be able to eliminate bottlenecks that have been hampering progress in the 1970s. Increased local participation should make it possible to extend programs more effectively into rural areas, where central-government personnel will always be scarce and under suspicion. Moreover, this improvement should have a multiplier effect, not only on family-planning work but also on all aspects of economic and social development. If indeed all of development is seen as a qualitative change, rather than merely a quantitative increase in gross national product, a decade more of administrative experience in the delivery of services to rural areas should have a great impact. The Malthusian rhetoric that reductions in population growth can be a substitute for economic and social programs and the opposing Bucharest rhetoric that population growth can be reduced by general economic and social programs will both be irrelevant. The major issue will be whether nations or communities can organize themselves to provide social services for their people in an equitable and effective manner.

Will voluntary services, information, and education be sufficient? Or will governments turn, like those of China and India, toward various types of pressures?

In Latin America, because birthrates are already responding to relatively small service programs, coercion seems out of the question. In Africa pronatalism still flourishes south of the Sahara. There, too, expanded services will be the approach acceptable to governments.

Only in Asia, where high population densities provide a constant and highly visible reminder of the problem, are governments likely to consider anything beyond voluntary services. Even there, national governments should hesitate before seeking to apply pressures beyond their administrative capacity, pressures that will be unpopular politically, and pressures more costly on a national basis than the extension of voluntary services. In the long run, in the developing countries as elsewhere, the most effective and acceptable forms of pressure on individuals to reduce fertility will come from the most immediate sources, from community or even family leaders who can identify and articulate a community or personal need better than the remote national government. These efforts will certainly be strongest in areas where everyone can see and appreciate the limits of land and resources that make constraints on population growth desirable. On islands such as Hong Kong, Taiwan, Java, Bali, Mauritius, and Sri Lanka, for example, the physical limits of land area are easily perceived even by simple villagers. Within larger countries, when villagers see that no more land is available in the countryside and that not enough jobs exist in the cities, then local leaders will be in a strong position to urge curbs on fertility. The role of the national government thus becomes one of lending its full support to local efforts, rather than one of sending in strangers to "motivate" illiterate villagers. In cultures where men and women do not now choose their own spouses but leave this crucial decision to family or village leaders, there is likely to be much less resentment over community, family, or even employer pressures to reduce fertility than there would be in the more individualistic societies of the Western world.

Thus, while incentives, disincentives, and various forms of social pressure to reduce fertility will be limited to countries and even areas within countries where overcrowding is patently visible to the population, by the 1980s voluntary family-planning services will be a familiar element in national policy. To put it another way, by the 1980s service programs designed specifically to modify fertility will be taken for granted by the developing world in much the same way that formal public education is taken for granted today by the developed world. The fertility problem itself will not be solved in the sense that no further government intervention or expenditure will be required. Everyone will not have a perfectly planned two-child family. But the policy problem will be resolved at the political level. No one will question the appropriateness of government policies to encourage low fertility and government support for family-planning programs designed to achieve it.

With respect to the legal changes and social policies that may indirectly contribute to lower fertility, the trend throughout the world is clearly toward further adoption of such measures. But with the possible exception of raising the age of marriage, there are at least three good reasons why, if these policies are adopted and implemented by governments, it will be primarily for purposes other than fertility control.

First, insofar as these indirect policies involve shifts in the social or economic power balance, as improving the status of women or land and tax reform clearly do, they will require strong political support from the population groups that expect to gain and from political leaders, who must respond to the pressures of their constituents. In some instances, leaders may be so powerful that they can disregard short-term opposition, but generally speaking political leaders are more likely to be moved by popular pressures than by academic evidence linking lower fertility with increased opportunities for women.

Furthermore, popular support for measures that may in fact

reduce fertility is rarely motivated by demographic concerns. The women's movement, for example, rejects the very concept of demographic impact as demeaning and manipulative. This is perfectly reasonable and proper. To seek to improve the economic and social status of women merely in order to reduce their fertility is, in effect, to continue to regard women primarily for their breeding—or in this case, nonbreeding—potential. Perhaps in an evolutionary biological sense it is true that sex roles must always adapt themselves in such a way as to ensure survival of the species, but from the relatively short-term view of government policies, it is social and individual, not biological, values that must justify national actions. In this context, the best reason to provide women with other opportunities in life besides childbearing is not to reduce fertility, or even to provide equality on an abstract basis, but rather to permit women, like men, to contribute to the primary challenge today—improving living conditions in their communities and nations. Societies that bar women from any such role outside their immediate families are depriving themselves of the useful service of half their populations.

In short, if support for improved status of women, more equitable distribution of income, or reductions in infant mortality becomes an important part of national policy—and this seems to be happening—it will and should be justified in the political arena for other than purely demographic reasons.

Second, many of the social policies that may indirectly affect fertility involve increased benefits for the entire population rather than just for those adults in their reproductive years. These policies, such as compulsory education, old-age security and improved health, will be very costly. The extent to which developing countries can afford them will depend on their natural resources, domestic economic policies, and international economic conditions ranging from the price of oil and other primary commodities to the magnitude of development assistance. Although better understanding of the demographic consequences of different policies may prove useful in setting development priorities among these programs, it is not likely that any expensive social program will be or should be undertaken exclusively or even primarily to reduce fertility. After all, one of the most persuasive arguments used in the 1960s in favor of initiating

137

family-planning programs was that they would cost very little compared with other development programs.

Third, to the extent that meaningful legal change and social policy depend on knowledge and experience, it is by no means clear that any of today's experts, including those in the West, know how to carry out such policies as land reform or income redistribution without sacrificing economic growth and political stability. Where, for example, is there a model among either developed or developing countries for an equitable tax structure that also promotes savings and investment necessary for economic growth? Who can say how land and other resources should be redistributed so as to guarantee self-sustaining economic development? What are the real opportunities for women in circumstances where male unemployment or underemployment is already high? Given the enormous gaps in knowledge about social and economic engineering, what government would embark upon such ambitious policies merely to lower the birthrate?

If this analysis is correct, if national government policies are to remain largely voluntary and service-oriented while smaller political or economic units take the lead in successfully testing or implementing more innovative or forceful measures, what should be the role of international agencies? Can population growth and fertility measures be handled as global issues at all and, if so, how?

As noted earlier, the initial impact of international agencies in identifying problems, projecting trends and solutions, and providing technical assistance to help national governments deal with population problems has not been negligible. For the future, there are at least four areas in which the role of the UN or other international agencies will continue to be significant.

First, multilateral agencies should continue to be a major source of financial and technical assistance to the poorest of the developing countries in extending services, training, and popular education. Although the United States was the first country to provide substantial assistance and still provides more than half of the $300 million to $350 million now available in international assistance, the UNFPA has become the major channel for government-to-government aid. The UNFPA will need a budget several times higher than the current $100 million level to meet increasing requests for help. USAID and UNFPA officials estimate that at least $500 million annually for the next 10 years could be put to good use. These funds should not, moreover, be restricted to foreign-exchange costs or commodities, as some bilateral assistance has been, but should be applied directly to reach those in greatest need for help. Nor should this assistance be limited to centralized national programs. Instead, the international agencies, like other donors, should seek out and support programs that grow from the grass roots upward, programs that involve not only government bureaucracies but also, and preferably, the men and women in thousands of villages who really determine their country's demographic future.

Second, the UN and the international donor community can provide much-needed channels for research into contraceptive techniques. Although the United States was a leader in developing the pill and perfecting and supplying other devices and equipment, government restrictions on new drug development and testing have slowed the pace of private pharmaceutical research in this country. At the same time, American congressional opposition to abortion-related activities and the use of injectable contraceptives have highlighted the need for international research in these specific areas. Moreover, other countries want more biomedical research conducted under local conditions in which their own scientists can play a larger role; international agencies can sponsor such research. Collaborative international research protocols can internationalize contraceptive evaluation and give greater legitimacy to new contraceptive methods.

Individual countries likewise want their professionals to play a larger role in social science research relating to population, and this type of research is the third area in which international agencies can be useful. Not only can they sponsor national efforts, but they can try to find answers to questions that national governments and aid donors need to know and cannot easily find: What social and economic policies will have the greatest influence on fertility patterns? Does development planning take full account of population-growth issues? What management skills are needed to improve service delivery?

Finally, the international agencies, with all their bureaucratic delays, politically motivated compromises, and internal inefficiencies, can raise the level of concern over population from a bilateral or purely national issue to a global concern. They can direct attention to the relationships between population growth and other economic and social issues. Even though they have not succeeded in earlier efforts to set precise international demographic goals, they are still able to assess national plans versus national accomplishments and project claims versus project results. Objective performance evaluation will not be easy for any intergovernmental bodies, but this function will have to be carried out if they are to retain the confidence of their own donors. Furthermore, international agencies can force their member governments to vote and take a position. They can, in effect, insist on various activities as a prerequisite for expanded assistance. Above all, by their very existence and operations they can reinforce the view that population problems, like environmental, food, and other development problems, are an international responsibility. Although the specific policies and programs to deal with population growth may be national, the repercussions of those programs will be international.

This involvement of international bodies will represent, on the one hand, a reasonable continuation and extension of their present roles. On the other hand, it will strengthen what must surely be considered a revolutionary trend toward interaction, not merely between international agencies and governments but also, and more important, between international agencies and communities or individuals. This new interaction has been implicit in the redefinition of development as a social rather than a purely economic process. It is implicit in the term *interdependence*. It is becoming explicit in the new appeals for international standards and action on human rights.

During the 1980s, growing global concern over population growth—which depends so fundamentally on individual actions—will surely reinforce this trend, and in turn, the population-growth policies of the 1980s will themselves be reinforced by this greater international activism.

FOUR

The Problem of Population Distribution in the 1980s

POPULATION DISTRIBUTION TRENDS IN THE 1980s

Regardless of what happens to fertility in the 1980s—whether, as anticipated here, birthrates fall from what could be called the danger levels, above 20 per thousand, or whether they remain stubbornly high for several decades—any government that wants to stay in power in the last two decades of the twentieth century will have to be concerned much more with the distribution and density of existing young, vigorous populations than with reducing the birthrate. There can be little doubt that once birthrates come down to about 20 per thousand, the major question confronting governments will be how to cope with the deferred impact of the demographic bulge. Like a river rising in flood, real demographic pressures and danger come not when heavy rains are falling in the mountains but when the waters reach their crest in a settled area.

The flood of young adults aged 15 to 30 that will crest in the developing countries in the 1980s will, as noted earlier, number nearly one billion out of a total world population of 3 billion to 3.5 billion (assuming a continuing decline in birthrates and thus a smaller cohort below age 15). Thus this energetic, volatile age group will constitute between a third and a fourth of the total world population.

Whereas children under 15 are politically impotent, that is, unable to make political claims against governments to improve their condition, young adults in the prime of life in numbers too large to find adequate education, employment, housing, or even in some cases food will be socially conspicious and politically demanding. This is the age group of maximum physical and mental energy. It is the age group most likely to be independent of its parents, yet without responsibility for dependents of its own. It is the age group most likely to migrate from the rural areas—where the opportunity to own or rent enough land to make a living is diminishing—to urban centers, where even at subsistence wages life in general is more varied and exciting. It is the age group in which young men, at least, are most likely to turn toward crime and violence to satisfy basic needs, psychological compulsions, or ideological beliefs. It is the age group most likely to heed appeals for revolutionary change in social and political structures. Finally, it is the age group that has grown up entirely in independent nations, free from colonial constraints and constantly exposed to nationalist exhortations and the rhetoric of raised expectations.

Were there new worlds to conquer, new continents to settle, even new factories waiting for workers, these young men and women might be able to build an adequate place for themselves and for their children. But today there are few new frontiers to settle, and industrial opportunities lag far behind the growth in rural and urban work forces. Moreover, at least three-quarters of the next generation will still have grown up in rural areas, where they will have received little training in skills suited for city life or for the technological needs of developing societies.

Nor will the past experience of Western industrial cities with rural and foreign migrants offer much guidance for policy in developing Third World cities. Because of the large numbers of migrants involved and the unprecedentedly strong "push" effect of rural overpopulation and poverty, a smaller proportion of migrants is likely to be of the self-selected, socially mobile type identified with earlier migrations.[40] More will be socially dis-

[40]David Turnshaw, *The Employment Problem in Less Developed Countries: A Review of Evidence*, Employment Series no. 1, Organization for Economic Cooperation and Development, Paris, 1971, pp. 41–43; Todaro, *Internal Migration*, pp. 15–46; Browning, "Migrant Selectivity," pp. 292–293.

advantaged—the rural unemployed, uneducated, and unskilled workers whose move to the cities will be prompted more by desperation than by hope. Furthermore, all migrants by the 1980s will have been more exposed to political activism than earlier generations: through the mass media and the example of growing numbers of urban and rural guerrillas, student demonstrators, and other protesters. Under conditions of growing unrest, aggravated by new masses of impoverished and dispossessed urban and rural populations, it will not be difficult to identify foreign scapegoats, to arouse great hostility toward the affluent countries, and to vent frustrations by sabotaging foreign interests and expropriating businesses, as well as kidnapping foreign business leaders, hijacking airplanes, and committing other terrorist acts. But the most accessible targets for all forms of local discontent and frustration will be the national leaders themselves. In relatively democratic societies, they will be highly vulnerable to divided governments and political repudiation. And in what may well be an increasing number of dictatorships, even the seemingly omnipotent leader will live in constant fear of coups d'état and assassination.

This potential for violence will be aggravated wherever different races, religions, tribes, or ethnic groups live in close juxtaposition. If these populations are growing rapidly, with large numbers of rootless young men on the move and limited opportunities for peaceful employment, conflict is almost inevitable. Wherever juxtaposed groups experience different fertility rates, the group with the highest per capita income and the greatest economic power is always the group with the lowest fertility. In these circumstances population growth represents a threat to the status quo: to political dominance and economic and social stability. This threat can easily erupt into a political crisis. When outbreaks do occur, of course, the immediate causes will always be perceived as political, but the underlying reasons may indeed be demographic.

POPULATION DISTRIBUTION POLICIES FOR THE 1980s

What should be the policy response of governments in the developing and developed world to this new, more populous, and more volatile generation?

Since the coming migration-employment crisis is inevitably one generation (15 to 20 years) behind the fertility crisis in its peak impact, policies to deal with it also lag a generation or so behind. And evaluation of those policies lags still further. Moreover, in migration, even more than in fertility, the issues are immensely complex. None of the broad range of population-distribution policies thus far attempted has been entirely effective, and most have been extremely expensive.

Of the five basic strategies mentioned earlier—rapid urbanization, modernization of agriculture, integrated rural development, dispersed urbanization, and regional development—the first two, which have essentially prevailed so far, will probably not be abandoned even though their results may be increasingly criticized. With regard to agriculture, the crucial need for food to supply growing populations will require maximizing output. Only if it can be proved in the circumstances of each country that small or labor-intensive farms can really produce as much as large, mechanized farms is there likely to be a serious concern over dispossessed smallholders. In other words, at the national level the short-term pressures for food will almost certainly override longer-term considerations of stable population distribution.

At the same time, the pressures for an activist role by the central government in promoting an expanding industrial base and encouraging export production to meet balance-of-payments problems will encourage continued growth of the capital city and major port and manufacturing cities. Moreover, just as high fertility now produces a young population and therefore continued high birthrates later, large-scale migration to capital cities produces an inevitable multiplication of urban services at the cost of rural development, which in turn encourages more rural-to-urban migration. The momentum already created may be impossible to halt voluntarily for several decades.

Experimental job-creation policies, such as integrated rural development, dispersed urbanization, and regional development, which seek to check rapid urbanization, will almost certainly be more widely adopted because governments will increasingly recognize the theoretical advantage of these approaches. Indeed, the issues of job creation and appropriate technology (including labor-intensive versus capital-intensive programs) are already receiving worldwide attention. But all such efforts require vast resources, extensive coordination of complex economic policies, and a very long-term commitment. Whether during the 1980s developing countries will have sufficient resources and administrative ability to put forth such efforts on a large enough scale to make a difference is questionable.

One of the most neglected resources in developing-country planning is the basic resilience and willingness to work of the average citizen. When government resources are lacking, national leadership should look to its own private citizens and nongovernmental organizations to apply the initiatives and find the energy that is needed. There is increasing evidence that even the poorest of the poor, even the socially disadvantaged migrants, can do a great deal to help themselves if minimal services and technical guidance are provided. This type of self-help has certainly been a significant factor in declining fertility. Basically, economic productivity, like fertility control, depends on the willingness of individuals to apply themselves and to take risks by changing traditional patterns of behavior. When governments are simply not able to find public funds to provide roads, housing, schools, health services, and factories in every present or potential population center, they can and should encourage individuals to build what is needed for themselves, providing sites, minimal services, basic credit, technical advice, and long-term government protection for their efforts.

National governments can also encourage additional initiatives by local groups—villages, cooperatives, agricultural schools, businesses, and organizations of all kinds—to work together to improve local conditions without looking to the national government as the only guide and leader. Governments can also avoid measures that discourage or hamper community or private

145

initiative, such as urban "removal" projects that break up viable squatter neighborhoods or cheap-food policies that reduce incentives to small farmers.

Almost certainly governments will look for ways to reinforce all forms of incentives and support programs by restrictions and coercive measures against those who fail to cooperate voluntarily. There is no denying that the most successful programs to control migration as well as to reduce fertility have been implemented by the People's Republic of China and some of the other communist countries not only through indirect benefits or incentives but also by more or less coercive means. For example, work brigades meet together to decide who will have babies each year. People who leave the countryside without authorization are denied ration cards in the city. The total organization of society to meet national goals makes it possible to apply such pressures very effectively at the local level. Most other developing countries, however, do not appear to have the political capacity or desire to implement either coercive migration or coercive fertility policies. Nevertheless, as population densities increase, all countries in the world will be moving toward more restrictive land-use and economic planning policies, especially for urban areas. These restraints, combined with fewer job opportunities in the cities and probably higher food prices, may slow the flow of migration somewhat. But even so, it is unlikely that by the 1980s many of the developing countries will be able to carry out land-use or other deliberate population-distribution policies in such a way as to check the continuing flow of migrants and job seekers into the major cities.

In dealing with these problems of internal migration and distribution, the role of the international community will be limited. As with fertility control programs, the rest of the world can provide some resources, some research, and some evaluation. The international business community can offer an added dimension by reviewing the impact of its operations; for example, corporations should deliberately encourage labor-intensive technology, insist on factory locations that will not add to urban congestion, and provide more on-the-job training for indigenous workers.

146

But the real force of international attention will focus on international, not internal, migration. By the 1980s, international migration will be a major issue. It will seem to some nations as important politically as their own national boundaries and as important economically as the price of their major commodity exports. (It will also represent a major impingement of some countries' population-growth problems upon other countries.)

International migration will certainly increase in numbers in the 1980s. The bulk of this migration will be from the developing countries to the developed countries. In fact, legal migration from Africa, Asia, and Latin America to Australia, Canada, and the United States doubled during the 1960s and will probably double again by the 1980s.[41] Western Hemisphere immigration, legal and illegal, into the United States from Mexico and the Caribbean will surely increase. Even now Mexico's annual population increase of 2 million (over a population base of 60 million) exceeds the U.S.A.'s increase of 1.7 million (over a population base of nearly 220 million). In fact, estimated illegal immigration into the United States of nearly 1 million annually, if accurate, almost equals the natural increase of present United States citizens.

Declining population growth in the developed countries will accelerate this trend. By the mid-1980s, the smaller number of developed-country births in the late 1960s will translate into smaller numbers of developed-country youth entering the workforce. Thus, there will be even more opportunities for immigrant workers at the lower and apprentice level of the labor market in the developed countries. In fact, there may be a substantial business demand for their services.

At the same time, migration from less to more prosperous developing countries will also swell. The oil-rich, population-scarce Arab countries will draw technicians from North Africa and South Asia. Within Latin America and Africa, migration to countries with jobs and resources will surely increase, straining already uneasy relationships.

For the hard-pressed national leaders of poorer nations facing

[41]UN, *International Migration Trends, 1950–1970*, Bucharest Population Conference Background Paper, May 22, 1974, (E/CONF.60/CBP/18), pp. 10–12.

the impossibility of keeping a multitude of young adults employed, satisfied, and not reproducing too rapidly, international migration will look more and more like a welcome safety valve. Even though the number of emigrants will not come close to the size of population increases at home, emigration will nonetheless offer the immediate benefits of removing some potential troublemakers, reducing domestic unemployment somewhat, and adding to foreign exchange through remittances sent home.

There are, of course, disadvantages to the country of origin. Because international migrants are usually more skilled or more enterprising than those who remain behind, they leave a gap, especially in fields such as science, medicine, and engineering. The developing countries are loath to lose these professionals and try to restrict their departures, but so far they have proved sufficiently clever and persistent to evade restrictions from their own countries. Even other types of immigrants, for example, guest workers who come from southern to northern Europe on a temporary basis or Pakistanis and Egyptians who find jobs in the Middle East, are semiskilled technicians who are able to adapt to new jobs quickly. Basically, they represent the cream of the labor force in their native countries. Is their departure really a boon to their homelands? Do the cash remittances they send home really compensate for the initial costs of raising and educating them and the later loss of their personal initiative and enterprise? Does their departure speed the fall of birthrates and encourage the remaining families, communities, and even nations to hasten the development process?

To each of these questions the emerging long-term answer is probably negative. Countries from which emigrants go have generally not prospered; cash remittances are no substitute for a viable national economy; and the stagnation that often follows massive emigration actually seems to delay declines in fertility and other elements of modernization.[42] Yet the countries from which migrants come tend to encourage emigration, and the countries where they settle are increasingly restricting it.

[42]Cf. Kingsley Davis, "The Migrations of Human Populations," *Scientific American*, September 3, 1974, pp. 93–105.

This will certainly continue to be true if the developed countries experience high unemployment, especially among present minority groups and young people, as may well be the case. The United States, for example, is already acting to curb illegal immigration and to limit the legal entry of physicians. Some of the affluent Third World countries, such as Venezuela, Nigeria, and Iran, may well follow suit in the 1980s. But despite legal barriers, wherever countries share long land borders or unpatrolled coasts and where a great disparity in living standards and economic opportunities persists, these efforts are bound to be costly and inefficient as well as diplomatically awkward.

Under these circumstances, in a decade when migration will inevitably increase, international migration policies will be under the same pressure as fertility and trade policies in the 1970s to move out of the strict context of national sovereignty and to take account of economic and social pressures. In other words, immigration and emigration policies will not long continue to escape the cry for social justice or a new international order. Yet at the same time the economic capacity of the developed world to produce jobs and the political capacity of any nation to absorb large, ethnically different, and highly nationalistic populations will decline. Nations will become ever more reluctant to grant the full rights of citizenship to overflow workers who retain close ties to another land and culture.

One possible compromise, consistent with the effort to place international migration policies in the context of economic and social development, is an expansion of the "guest worker" arrangements already existing in Western Europe. Instead of searching as individuals for employment in modern industry, guest workers, like Peace Corps volunteers in reverse, could sign up for a fixed period of service and then be required to return to their countries of origin.

Just as developed countries provide assistance to the governments of developing countries, the public and private sectors of developed countries should assume a responsibility to train developing-country guest workers in rudimentary agriculture, business, mechanics, or other work and perhaps set aside a monthly cash allowance that will be available only at the scheduled date of departure. Over the long term, the migrants could accumulate skills, capital, and some experience in a developed-country economic environment. Indeed, more can be learned by more people in this way than by sending one or two developed-country technicians overseas.

Upon their return after a specified period, migrants should look to their own countries, assisted by international agencies, to help them find similar productive employment at home. As with urban squatters, they might be provided with some of the sites and services they need, so that they could build homes for themselves or establish businesses. In this way the experience of migration would not be a net loss to the developing country, but a long-term gain. Moreover, families, communities, and nations would not be able to find in migration an escape from the basic planetary need to balance population and resources.

In short, the time is rapidly coming when international migration policies will no longer be considered almost a substitute for indigenous development, just as birth control is no longer viewed as a substitute for social and economic policies. International migration policies, like fertility policies before them, will have to come of age during the 1980s, with no less controversy and perhaps even more nationalist rhetoric and diplomatic wrangling. As governments of emigrating workers seek to derive greater development benefits from the export of their "best and brightest," governments on the receiving end will be under great pressure to replace the negative and restrictive elements of historic immigration policies with a more constructive, development-oriented combination of services and regulations.

To develop standards for such migrants and to monitor national compliance, an international organization may have to be established or strengthened. Its role would be to deal with or for individuals and groups as well as sovereign governments. It could be expected to seek resources and even to apply these resources for the express purpose of helping to integrate migration into economic and social planning.

In policies of population distribution, as in policies relating to human reproduction, the basic issue is the same. The question is both moral and practical. To what extent should a government's policies depend primarily on a rational individual's assessment of his or her best interests, influenced by whatever positive economic incentives or supporting social services that government can realistically provide? And to what extent must a government turn toward negative controls, restricting individual freedom in the interests of the community or nation? This is, of course, a basic dilemma of government in all areas of operation, but where individual freedom to reproduce or move about at will is at stake, the dilemma is especially agonizing to the liberal conscience of the West.

The fact is that in highly developed Western societies, governments have so far been able to keep population growth and distribution in rough balance by providing a broad array of social services and a fairly narrow range of restrictions on personal freedom. This approach is consistent with Western values and remains the only approach to social control that is a proven vote getter in countries with regular elections.

In the relatively developed communist countries, the emphasis is different. Governments have imposed severe restrictions on personal mobility (although not on fertility) and have moved rapidly to provide an extremely broad range of social and economic services. This approach has been tolerated by those living under it largely because it is backed by military force combined with real improvements in the standard of living.

In the less developed areas, however, most governments cannot afford to provide enough supportive services and incentives to eliminate excess fertility immediately or to control population distribution. Most of them also lack sufficient political or administrative authority to enforce prohibitions against large families or curbs on personal mobility in an equitable or efficient way.

Thus, during the 1980s, these governments are likely to move haltingly in both directions. To the extent that supportive services and incentives require resources and technical guidance, the developed nations can and should help. In the long run, the ability of developing countries to meet the basic needs of their citizens will be the best guarantee in all fields of voluntary programs that do not violate human rights. On the other hand, to the extent that resources, technical skills, and managerial abilities fall short, the temptation, even the need, to use coercion will be hard for some governments to resist. Even if this becomes necessary, however, and the human values of the Western world are sometimes sacrificed, overwhelmed by the very number and intransigence of human beings, the most effective population policies, as well as those most acceptable to all peoples—involving efforts to integrate a new, larger, more spatially mobile younger generation into useful social and economic roles—will be based on maximum voluntary participation and minimum external restrictions.

If the demographic crises of the 1980s and 1990s are surmounted, then finding place for a smaller population increase that will follow in later decades should not be so difficult. But where governments cannot control or cope with their vastly increased citizenry, serious social disorganization may develop nationally or even internationally. Indeed, precipitated by political, religious, or racial disputes, such disorganization may be inevitable and may already have begun in parts of the Middle East, Central America, and South Asia. Whether most nations of the world will emerge from the period of turmoil socially integrated, economically prosperous, and politically stable in the 1990s will depend to a very great extent on how policies of population growth and distribution are implemented and how these policies are coordinated with development programs to assure increasing economic and social opportunity for the coming generation.

Demographic Projections:
A Critical Evaluation

Georges Tapinos

ONE

A Panorama of Demographic Projections

THE NATURE OF DEMOGRAPHIC PROJECTIONS

What are demographic projections? The diversity of jargon is the first sign of ambiguity. *Forecasts, projections, future prospects, predictions, demographic futures, demographic perspectives* are among the terms one hears, and there are many more. What accounts for this profusion of vocabulary? Are the terms merely synonyms, by-products of the fad of "forecasting" and the linguistic ingenuity of demographers, or are they a manifestation of the variety of concepts that can in fact be applied to different phenomena? A traditional distinction contrasts *projections*—calculations involving demographic variables only, e.g., age-specific birth- and death rates—with *forecasts*, which take into account socioeconomic variables, e.g., the changing status of women. This distinction reflects the belief of many demographers that calculating the evolution of a population is a rather technical operation, requiring strictly neutral procedures. But in fact, calculating a population's rate of growth necessitates the use of certain hypotheses, especially about fertility rates, that are not purely statistical.

Any projection begins with an extrapolation; the most accurate extrapolations are those that account for all variables except possible changes in human attitudes that produce changes in behavior. But even such accurate extrapolations have inherent difficulties of their own. In order to project certain trends one must first define the past period to be taken as a base. In using only the immediate past (which one does not always know with great precision), anomalous aberrations may be mistaken for the norm. By focusing too far back in the past, one may not give sufficient weight to permanent shifts that occurred more recently and thus inaccurately forecast the short-term future.

Initially, forecasts of population growth were nothing more than simple geometric projections of seemingly constant growth rates observed in the past for entire populations. Thomas Malthus (1766–1834) is most frequently associated with such exercises, although others preceded him in this realm. Throughout the nineteenth century, the compound-interest formula was the principal method used in calculating future population growth rates, with certain more refined methods, such as those of the Belgian statistician Adolphe Quételet, used only rarely. In the twentieth century, this crude approach gave way to the so-called component method, whose application requires knowledge not only of the size of a population but also of its age structure and its age-specific fertility and mortality rates. The new information provided by this method of calculation permits much more refined projections. What is emphasized in effect is not so much the total size of the population, but its various demographic structures and their socioeconomic implications.

In general, projections are first calculated on the national level (total population and its distribution according to age and sex). From these primary facts information is derived concerning the work force, the school-age population, the number of retired people, and the like. By applying certain hypotheses—especially those on internal migration—one can determine the distribution of population between cities and rural areas and more generally, the regional distribution of the population. This latter determination is very important because, as Hoem emphasized, "restriction to the national level sometimes obscures many of the complexities involved,"[1] although coherently synthesizing different regional projections into a national projection is a particularly complex problem.

[1] J. M. Hoem, "Levels of Error in Population Forecasts," *Artikler*, no. 61, 1973, p. 46.

THE AIMS OF DEMOGRAPHIC PROJECTIONS

There are at least two reasons for the development of demographic projections. The first is immediate and well known. The size of a population, its age structure, and the factors causing these to vary provide the basis for a whole series of social and economic indicators—school-age population, new housing, dependency ratio, costs of social security benefits, etc.—the knowledge of which is indispensable to political and economic decision making.

But more important, there is the "technocratic rationale": a quantitative presentation of the future is important as a means of influencing public opinion. A projection, even if it is unrealistic, by demonstrating "what will happen if things continue as they are," can influence public opinion and thereby facilitate the adoption of corrective measures by public authorities. For example, the first demographic projections carried out in France between the First and Second World Wars painted a picture of a nation that had become much older and much reduced in size and thus incontestably played a bogeyman role. The doomsday projections did not predict the actual evolution of the population; rather they modified it by making the French people aware of adverse demographic phenomena and thus facilitated the adoption of policies to increase fertility. Conversely, when projected trends coincide with the way the public would like society to evolve, people will tend to act as though the projections are admonitions, which will have the effect of harmonizing the real evolution of the population with its projected evolution. These influences are what certain demographers have called "publication effects."

In the case of the doomsday projections of world population made by many organizations, such as the Club of Rome, behavioral change is intentionally sought. It is believed that one means of slowing demographic growth is to present to the public at large the image of an overpopulated future world in which demographic pressures would be intolerable. But confusing the descriptive and admonitory nature of projections can have effects different than those desired. For example, when a country wants to slow down the growth of its population and takes family-planning measures to this end, the demographic projections it calculates take into account not only tendencies observed in the past but also the probable evolution of the population based on the assumption that the regulatory policies adopted will be effective; however, experience demonstrates that certain countries have confused their hopes with reality.

Major surprises concerning projections of fertility in developed countries are significant in this regard. In the 1930s, the decline in fertility reached a point at which—in some cases—replacing the population in the future was no longer assured. To maintain a steady-state population, according to demographers, would have required a certain proportion of families with four or five children, to compensate for the inevitable number of single people, sterile couples, and couples with a single child. And it was generally recognized as unlikely that there would be a sufficient number of such families. But the facts—the post–World War II "baby boom"—contradicted these predictions.[2] This boom did not lack for explanations: The average age of marriage had been reduced, and the proportion of permanently nonmarried people had been reduced by about 10 percent. Simple extrapolation of these new tendencies led to predictions of sizable growth in population. But these new predictions were also contradicted by events. After 1964–1965, fertility declined in most of the developed countries. Since that time, burned by their earlier forecasts, demographers have become more prudent. They have tried to measure the scope and nature of declining fertility without putting forward too many detailed predictions. But they have reached one conclusion: The need to have a proportion of large families in order to maintain a steady-state population is no longer regarded as important.

[2]See C. F. Westhoff, "The Populations of the Developed Countries," *Scientific American*, vol. 231, no. 3, September 1974. According to Westhoff, at the beginning of World War II the population of the developed countries at the time (i.e., Europe including the Soviet Union, North America, Australia, and New Zealand) was about 720 million. Demographic projections foresaw a population of 845 million in these societies today, but it is in fact now 940 million.

In spite of all this, medium- and long-range demographic projections are generally the most reliable ones in the social sciences. However, as Figure 1 illustrates, as the length of the time horizon increases, the level of confidence we can have in age-specific projections declines.[3] Nevertheless, it is wrong always to assume that the shorter the time horizon, the smaller the margin of error. For any given period the accuracy of a forecast depends on the demographic factors being considered.

Demographic projections are based on two types of phenomena: the inertia of population structures (such as the size of the labor force or the number of retired people) and the stability of behavior. If the birthrate were to drop to 0 tomorrow morning, this would have little effect on the size of the working population before a period of about 20 years. But it is a highly improbable hypothesis, not to say a practical impossibility, that men and women married in say, 1977 would decide to have no children at all while those married the year before wanted two or three.[4] And even if the birthrate were to drop abruptly today, were to stay very low for 20 years, and then were to start rising, it would take a rather long time for the rising birthrate to make its effects felt. In other words, changes in behavior affecting fertility generally occur rather slowly, and their impact on population structures is delayed. That is why "demographic policy"—effective as voluntary and individual changes in behavior may be—should be developed and implemented as far in advance as possible in order that the desired effects may be achieved in time. This is one of the arguments in favor of making demographic projections.

---

[3]The multiplication of demographic projections and their contradictions by observed events have produced an abundance of literature on the sources of errors in projections and many typologies have been proposed. We may cite, among others, Hoem, "Levels of Error," and Nathan Keyfitz, "On Future Population," *Journal of the American Statistical Association*, vol. 67, no. 338, June 1972, pp. 347–363.

[4]Violent fluctuations do occasionally occur, but they are invariably short-term and transitory. The example of Japan in 1966 is well known: the total fertility rate from 1965 to 1966 to 1967 went from 2.1 to 1.6 to 2.2. Rumania's total fertility rate underwent a similar short-term evolution.

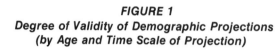

FIGURE 1
Degree of Validity of Demographic Projections
(by Age and Time Scale of Projection)

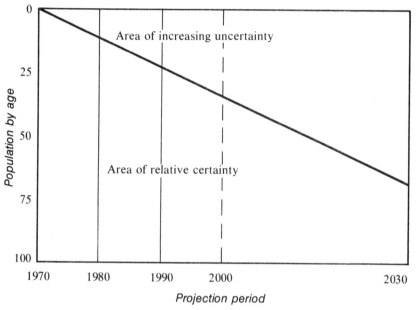

SOURCE: UN, *Economic Survey of Europe in 1974, Postwar Demographic Trends in Europe and the Outlook Until 2000*, New York, 1975, (ESA/P/AC. 5/2), vol. 2.

Mortality rates—which will be discussed in the next chapter—can be predicted accurately over a longer term than population structures. Population structures are basically predictable 20 years in advance, since most of the people involved are already alive as of the first year of the projection. However, predicting fertility rates is extremely tricky, both for the short term and for the long term—not only because it is difficult to predict the existence of something that has not yet appeared but also because fertility is above all a behavioral phenomenon. Since fertility rates are the determining element in population growth rates, this presents a problem. However, these rates hardly affect population structures in the short term.

TWO

Critical Evaluation of Existing Projections and Hypotheses

EXISTING PERSPECTIVES AND THEIR GENERAL CHARACTERISTICS

For some 20 years, the Population Division of the Department of Economic and Social Affairs of the UN has made population projections for every country in the world, generally for five-year periods but occasionally for different periods (see Bibliography). These principal projections serve as the basis for various derivative projections, such as the number of school-age children or the size of the labor force. Different agencies of the UN—mainly the International Labor Organization, the Food and Agricultural Organization, and the UN Economic and Social Council (UNESCO)—specialize in making derivative projections in order to assure both an effective division of labor and a general coherence for all the different calculations.

In this essay and the first one in this volume, I have primarily used the latest available UN projections, which were made in 1973, were published in 1977, and take into account new information revealed by numerous censuses made in 1970. In certain cases where the derivative projections are still lacking, I have had to use projections published at the Bucharest conference in 1974 that use 1968 as a base year.

The latest UN projections, entitled *World Population Prospects 1970–2000, as Assessed in 1973*, take 1970 as the base year and deal with the period 1970–2000. Through retrospective calculations, population figures for the period 1950–1970 are also included. These projections cover 242 countries or regions (with some redundancy) and present 26 demographic indicators for 187 of them. The 26 indicators are shown in the table for China in the first essay of this volume (see Table 9, pp. 52–55).

In addition to the projections made by the UN and its specialized agencies, projections for certain groups of countries, as well as for the entire world, are occasionally made by certain national and international bodies, most notably the Population Council, the U.S. Bureau of the Census, and the World Bank (see Bibliography).

In 1973, Tomas Frejka of the Population Council made projections of the world population based on an original methodology (see Bibliography). He tried to determine the level at which the population of various countries would stabilize depending upon when the average couple started having no more than two children.

The U.S. Bureau of the Census is interested principally in the United States, but its international section occasionally makes projections for certain less developed countries (especially India, Mexico, Colombia, Chile and other Latin American countries, Tunisia, and Thailand) to be used by the Agency for International Development. As a general rule, though, the Bureau does not carry out projections for the entire world or even for multinational geographical regions. Its demographic profiles for specific countries, however, constitute an excellent source of information because its fertility hypotheses are not determined by statistical methods alone, but take into account all relevant data available (in particular, surveys on what is considered by the population to be the ideal family size). In practice, the results obtained are fairly close to those of the medium variant of the UN, but they have the advantage of being based on a single theory of fertility, which reduces the arbitrary nature of the choice of variants.

The World Bank also develops its own projections—when it has to analyze the demographic and economic situation of a country whose government asks for credit—but generally it uses the projections of the UN. In 1972, it developed some projections for all its member countries in order to update UN projections for 1968, when the results of the 1973 series were not available.

The quality of information necessary for developing forecasts obviously affects their reliability. We do not have space here to summarize all the well-known deficiencies that, especially in the less developed world, reduce the accuracy of censuses and of information on civilians' status. It is useful, however, to note that for several countries in the world such information is classified by the UN as "approximate," "rough," or "very rough," and for China it is virtually nonexistent.

To what extent does the Population Division rely on national projections? The accuracy of national projections for some countries cannot be disputed, and in such cases the Population Division simply uses them (making only those adjustments necessary to ensure conformity with other data for the reference years). This is the procedure with respect to several developed countries; and with regard to Latin America, the UN simply uses the projections calculated by the Centro Latinoamerico de Demografía (CELADE). However, for many other countries, national projections do not seem to be of sufficiently good quality or, more often, there are no national projections at all. In these cases, the Division makes all the calculations itself, after doing its own data collection and verification—which is the most difficult part.

The criteria used by the UN in classifying countries as "developed" or "underdeveloped" result from multivariate analysis. But as one can see in the discussion of this problem in *Population Bulletin of the United Nations #7, 1963*, demographic indicators (and in particular gross reproduction rates) are generally the most important variables. The developed countries, according to the Population Division, include all of Europe (the Soviet Union too), North America, Australia, New Zealand, temperate Latin America (Argentina, Chile, Uruguay), and Japan. Why Israel is placed among the underdeveloped countries, while temperate Latin America and certain southern European countries (e.g., Albania) are classed as developed is difficult to explain. The main reason seems to be a practical one: A country's classification remains the same for the entire period covered by the projections, even though its status may have changed by that period's end.

EVALUATION OF HYPOTHESES

The UN projections drawn up in 1973, the first results of which have recently been published, have not yet been analyzed critically. They are, however, rather like the 1968 projections in general character, so that certain criticisms that were addressed to the earlier projections might be raised again.

It is difficult to criticize the techniques used, except at a very general level. Some people have criticized the UN, sometimes without justification, for submitting too far to the influence of Third World countries and for being too pessimistic in its view of their prospects. A perhaps more justifiable complaint is that the UN too often accepts without critical examination the projections made by each of the member countries. The UN has responded that the demographic services of any country are generally the sources of the most realistic hypotheses for studies of that country.

The UN's Hypotheses on Fertility

The UN's 1968 projections (base year 1965) were calculated at a time when the evolution of fertility in both the developed and the less developed countries was uncertain. In the developed countries a certain stabilization, indeed a slight decline in the fertility level, had begun to appear, but the phenomenon was too recent and its scope too small to judge whether it represented a long-term trend, i.e., a new behavioral pattern that would lead ultimately to a permanent decline, or a short-term aberration linked to a temporary change in families' scheduling of births. Between the periods 1950–1955 and 1960–1965, the gross reproduction rate for all developed countries fell from 1.4 to 1.35, which was too small a reduction upon which to base any reliable conclusions. In the case of the less developed countries, uncertainty stemmed not so much from difficulties in interpreting the cross-sectional indicators as from the mediocre quality of the data for a large majority of the countries involved. However, thanks to more recent studies and the increase in available data, deriving in particular from the censuses taken in the early 1970s, more accurate analyses could be made, and a new series of projections was carried out in 1973.

The explanatory model upon which these new projections are founded relies on the theory of demographic transition and is based on three postulates: (1) Fertility levels depend on economic and social conditions as well as on death rates; a corollary to this postulate is that to the degree socioeconomic development takes place and death rates decrease, the fertility rate must decrease. (2) Reduction in fertility takes place in stages—slow at the beginning, then accelerating, then slowing down again. More precisely, the intermediate phase of accelerated decline is the period from the time when a gross reproduction rate of 2.5 is reached to the time when a rate of 1.5 is achieved. (3) The final level at which fertility must stabilize corresponds to a net reproduction rate of 1. The rapidity with which this level is attained depends on the society; certain developed countries now approach it, while many less developed countries have no chance of reaching it before the end of this century.

The Population Division of the UN is forced to go beyond this general framework in order to take into account specific national patterns that stem from recent or long-term demographic trends. Even if one could assume that there is in all countries a long-run tendency toward reduction in family size, the rate of reduction and the underlying factors that determine it would vary from country to country, and so it would be impossible to create a single, simple model. This is why the Population Division has preferred to break down its projections of fertility into a battery of models, which classify the future trends in northwest Europe, Western Europe, southern Europe, North America, the U.S.S.R., Japan, Asia, Africa, the Arab countries, and Latin America.

In addition, in order to take into account the determinant role of fertility in demographic projections and the uncertainty about its most probable development, there is a tendency to increase the number of hypotheses used in making calculations. Thus, the UN uses four variants for fertility: medium, high, low, and constant. The constant variant extends the rates observed in 1970; the others assume fertility at various rates. Fertility is generally measured by the gross reproduction rate, the crude birthrate, the total fertility rate, and the general fertility rate. The gross reproduction rates that correspond to the UN's four variants in its 1973 projections are shown in Table 1.

The multiplication of hypotheses, which is simplified by the use of the computers, certainly increases the information available, but creates many problems as well. While it does facilitate an exploration of all possible cases that are reasonably likely to occur, it does not in itself improve the predictive validity of a

TABLE 1
Fertility Assumptions (Gross Reproduction Rate)

	1970–1975	1975–1980	1980–1985	1985–1990	1990–1995	1995–2000
More developed regions						
Medium	1.13	1.10	1.10	1.09	1.09	1.09
High	1.17	1.19	1.22	1.24	1.24	1.24
Low	1.11	1.03	1.00	0.97	0.97	0.96
Constant	1.16	1.16	1.16	1.17	1.17	1.17
Less developed regions						
Medium	2.57	2.46	2.30	2.11	1.94	1.75
High	2.62	2.54	2.44	2.32	2.18	2.00
Low	2.51	2.33	2.12	1.94	1.72	1.52
Constant	2.63	2.63	2.65	2.66	2.67	2.68

SOURCE: UN, Department of Economic and Social Affairs, Population Division, *Population Prospects as Assessed in 1973*, (ST/ESA/Ser. A60), pp. 128, 131, 134.

model. The availability of multiple projections does, however, facilitate comparisons of the evolution of two or more countries' population. (For example, based on a certain initial situation, one can see what will occur over a given time period if the American population follows a low variant and Mexico a high variant. See Table 11 of the first essay in this volume, p. 73.)

The choice of fertility variants has a determining role in demographic projections because the evolution of a population depends largely on fertility and because, through "compound-interest" effects, a slight difference between two variants can lead to rather important differences at the end of a projection's time horizon.

There is a major problem in correctly estimating recent trends and the present situation. The overall fertility characteristics of a generation of women can be known definitely only at the end of the childbearing period. It might be possible to extrapolate from partial information presently available (in practice, the fertility level reached by age 30 is a good enough basis for extrapolating the final level), but it would seem to be simpler to characterize fertility by calculating the risk during a specific period. However, at a given moment in time, the period rate could just as easily constitute a radical departure from the final level as a correct approximation of it.[5] Therefore the period rate can be used as an indicator of the final level of fertility only on the condition that fertility behavior remains *stable*. But it does not, and hence it is necessary to have ample information on past and present trends in order to make projections. The apparent fertility at any point in time can be changed

[5]Calculating period rates relates in the long term to longitudinal measures. If women in successive generations follow the same fertility patterns, it is clear that the period rate will be identical with the longitudinal index; conversely, if fertility behavior changes from one generation to another, the period rate will reflect the longitudinal index inaccurately. If change is unidirectional, as is the case for mortality (which has hardly had any reversals), one might, by using certain hypotheses, make corrections in the period rate. If, on the contrary, fertility undergoes fluctuating changes, the period rate does not provide any information concerning real behavior and risks the introduction of substantial errors. It could be the case that the period rate and the longitudinal index (which one will know after a while) are divergent.

either because the total number of children a woman has in her childbearing years varies or because the timing of the births of these children varies. A change in the fertility rate can reflect the same incidence of births coupled with a prolongation of the scheduling of births, a lower incidence without change in the scheduling, or a lower incidence with more-spread-out scheduling of births. (One can exclude the case of higher incidence accompanied by a very different pattern of scheduling of births, which is conceivable only as a result of specific disturbances, such as a war.) Thus, changes in the period rate are more important than changes in the cohort rate, which is the result of a rather regular evolution.

We have dwelt upon this technical aspect of fertility precisely because, as mentioned earlier, for several years now changes in fertility indicators have been observed in both developed and less developed countries. Demographic projections differ radically according to the interpretation given to these changes.

Fertility in the Developed Countries

Recent changes in fertility in the developed countries have removed a doubt that plagued earlier projections, but have also led to a new problem. There is now no longer any doubt that the reduction in fertility observed in 1964–1965 is part of a more general phenomenon affecting all developed countries, regardless of differences in culture or political regime. (East and West Germany, in spite of the number of ways in which they differ from one another, have undergone comparable evolutionary patterns, providing the most striking example.) And there is also no doubt that the downturn—of which the baby boom was only an aberration—reflects a fundamental long-term trend.

If forecasters are reassured on this point, they are nonetheless immediately confronted with a new problem. While there is agreement that fertility rates have been reduced, it is not clear how far this reduction will go. In certain countries fertility seems to have already dropped below the replacement level, and if one extrapolates recent trends in other countries, many of them will be in an identical situation in the near future, with the number of deaths exceeding the number of births. In other words, the extrapolation of recent trends leads to the projection of natural increase rates lower than ever observed in the past. Obviously, while one is always hesitant to think about radically new developments, the lack of historical precedent is not a sufficient reason to say something cannot happen in the future. But population growth cannot decrease infinitely, for the population in question would completely disappear. The problem is thus to calculate the most probable limit to the reduction in fertility rates.

A first approach would be to look to public opinion, which, as mentioned earlier, plays a very important role in demographic behavior. It is certain, for example, that the announcement by a country of an annual demographic balance in which deaths exceeded births would impress public opinion, but the change in attitudes that might then result would come too late to correct the immediate situation and would have effects felt only in the long-term future.

It might be more realistic to consider the economic implications of a population that would become, as a whole, older because of reduced fertility rates. The effect of this change in age structures on pension plans has already been discussed. But even if responsible authorities were well aware of the situation, individual fertility behavior would not necessarily change unless a perfectly efficient demographic policy to increase the birthrate were possible.

A much more plausible basis of calculation is the fact that in the developed countries the model of a two-child family is becoming the norm. Not only is a family with two children considered to be ideal, but the deviation around this average figure is, in fact, being reduced. To give an approximation of what is actually happening: The fertility rate is being reduced from about 2.5 toward 2 children per woman. This figure represents, of course, an average for the entire population. As the model family of two children progressively replaces the three-child model assumed to have existed previously, the number of families with two children, which was small when the index was about 2.5, will increase progressively until the two-child family becomes characteristic of a majority of couples. If the rate now falls to

1.9 children per couple, it will not necessarily be the case that a new state—leading to a one-child-family model—has begun, but rather that the model of the two-child family has, for all practical purposes, been generalized to the entire population. Sterile couples and a certain inevitable proportion of unmarried persons will account for the rate being below 2.1 or 2.0. In such an instance, the figure of 1.9 will not be interpreted as an intermediate stage in a decreasing trend going successively from 2.5 to 2.0 to 1.9 to 1.7, etc., but rather as a lower limit hardly likely to be passed.

Given the fact that perception of ideal family size now seems to correspond with the statistics, and that birth control techniques are more effective than in the past, it is increasingly likely that the number of children couples want and the number they actually have will correspond more closely in the future than they did in the past. This means that the growth rate of the developed world's population will be very close to, if not perhaps slightly below, the replacement level. It also means that government measures to increase birthrates, so that growth stays at replacement level, will probably be effective, given the narrowness of the gap to be overcome.

However, contraception is never 100 percent effective, and nothing guarantees that the behavior of couples will be stable over the course of a generation or across successive generations. In fact, some people reject the thesis that the present decline in fertility norms represents an irreversible long-term trend, believing instead that fertility norms are cyclical in character and that while there will not be a wholesale return to large families (in view of the new social status of women), there will be an increase in the number of children in the years to come. This argument is based on the belief that there is an interaction mechanism operating among fertility, economic conditions, and the labor market: About 15 to 20 years after the birthrate is increased, strong pressure on the labor market develops, which has a depressive effect on fertility; after another lag of 20 to 25 years, a much less populous generation reaches the labor market and reduces the economic pressures, thereby creating a climate more favorable to an increase in birthrates.

This summary of the argument oversimplifies things, and the process is not in fact as mechanistic as it sounds. However, the argument does emphasize essential weaknesses in the traditional methods of calculation for developed countries. Attributing to each age cohort a specific fertility behavior that is independent of changing economic and labor market conditions—as is generally done—leads to the expectation of continuously increasing (or decreasing) birthrates by virtue of the growth (or decline) in the size of the population. Projecting population growth on the basis of present structures and a table of age-specific birthrates, as the UN does, results in a linear extrapolation for a phenomenon that might be by nature cyclical.

Fertility in the Less Developed Countries

It is the evolution of fertility in the less developed countries that will remain the central problem in the demographic situation of the world over the next few decades. The problem posed is one that involves the interrelationship between demographic and economic variables, insofar as a reduction in fertility is associated with an improvement in economic conditions. One is confronted in this area with two contradictory propositions: On the one hand, the slowing down (or curbing) of demographic growth seems to be a prerequisite to economic take-off; on the other hand, the reduction of demographic growth seems to be possible only after an economic take-off has begun.

At first it was thought that birth control constituted a necessary precondition to any economic take-off and that new birth control techniques would work effectively to lower fertility. But the high hopes placed in these new techniques proved excessive. Certainly, the discovery of modern contraceptive devices constitutes a major innovation; though contraceptive practices have been known for a long time, newer ones have a higher level of effectiveness, a lower cost, and are more widely dispersed. Until recently, the traditional view was that the results in the larger countries that focused on family planning programs were disappointing, though not negligible (see, for example, the discussion on India in the first essay). With the exception of China, about

171

which it is difficult to make clear statements, the successful countries and regions involved (Korea, Taiwan, Hong Kong, western Malaysia, Singapore, Barbados, Chile, Costa Rica, Cuba, Jamaica, Trinidad and Tobago, Puerto Rico, Mauritius, Réunion, Tunisia, and Sri Lanka) were small in general, and their growth, under any hypothesis, had a limited effect on world population. Failures in family planning programs led to the realization that controlling fertility was not ultimately a question of the effectiveness of the *techniques* used but of the *acceptance* by the public of the policies recommended. In this regard, the 1974 Bucharest conference marked a radical change in the traditional approach. Several countries emphasized problems of development, especially inequalities in development, which they considered to be priority policy targets.

More recent data (covering the period 1965–1975) show that not only have the previously mentioned countries accelerated their fertility decline, but also certain large countries (India, Indonesia, Thailand, Philippines, Turkey, Egypt, Brazil, Colombia, Mexico, amongt others) have now started to undergo a similar decline.[6]

The fact is, however, that in spite of numerous empirical and theoretical studies, we do not really know exactly what affects fertility. Many factors seem to play a role: mortality, in particular infant mortality; living conditions and income distribution; education and women's status. Yet none of these factors is necessary and determinant in and of itself.

As Coale has emphasized, an examination of demographic history suggests that "education efforts can be more easily conceived and applied in certain cultures than in others." Chinese-based cultures in particular seem to be more receptive to efforts at reducing fertility. Coale has observed that in East Asia reductions in fertility have been effective in Japan, Korea, Taiwan, Hong Kong, western Malaysia, and Singapore. For these two last areas, the reduction has been limited to or most significant among the Chinese.[7] It is thus supposed that fertility is also

[6]See W. Parker Mauldin, "Patterns of Fertility Decline in Developing Countries, 1950–1975," *Studies in Family Planning*, vol. 9, no. 6, April 1978.

[7]Ansley Coale, "The Demographic Transition Reconsidered," in *International Population Conference, Liège, 1973*, International Union for the Scientific Study of Population, Liège, Belgium, vol. 1, 1974, pp. 53-72.

declining in China itself. However, the countries of so-called Chinese culture where fertility has declined are, in general, small in size; and the political regime in China probably has unique effects on the outcome of policies there. Thus the transferability of the Chinese experience is difficult to prove.

More generally, Habakkuk has observed that "in several regions in the underdeveloped world, social institutions are not well adapted for transforming demographic pressure into individual desires to reduce birth rates." He makes the following argument: In most of the countries under consideration, the family is a very large entity that is able to assume the burden of educating children because its various units share the costs; the marital age depends less on economic factors than is the case in Europe and is therefore lower, and the reduction in mortality has, with certain exceptions, not led to a reduction in fertility.[8]

In any case, the demographic cards have already been played for 1980–1990. However, what happens over the course of the next 20 years will have a determining effect on the world's long-term future. A reduction in fertility in the less developed countries as a whole is likely. Not excluded, however, is the likelihood that in certain countries an increase in fertility brought about by declining infant mortality and female mortality in the procreative ages will be revealed between now and 1990. But whatever the fertility rate, demographic structures in these countries will scarcely be affected, and the population will continue to grow.

The UN's Hypotheses on Mortality

In most demographic projections, much less attention is given to the evolution of mortality than to the analysis of fertility. There are two reasons for this relative lack of interest. First, the evolution of a population—its rate of growth and changes in its structures—depends more on fertility than on mortality, as analysis of quasi-stable populations has verified. Second, the study of past demographic patterns suggests that mortality evolved along a rather stable, if not entirely regular, path.

[8]H. J. Habakkuk, *Population Growth and Economic Development Since 1750*, Leicester University Press, Leicester, England, 1971, p. 85.

Practically all mortality projections are based on the following assumptions: (1) Life expectancy can only increase or stabilize, but cannot decrease. (2) It cannot increase indefinitely; there is a limit to average life expectancy. (3) There is a gap in the life expectancy of men and women that favors the latter, and this gap will remain more or less constant, perhaps even widening slightly. (4) One takes as a given a rate of change in life expectancy that is expressed in numbers of years or in months gained annually.[9] The UN Population Division calculates this rate by taking into account both actual observed limits on mortality and potential limits given the present state of medical knowledge.

The UN's 1973 projections also take into account an overestimation of the rate of growth in life expectancy made in earlier projections. As outlined in Table 2, the UN's medium-variant mortality hypothesis can be summarized as follows: The level of mortality in terms of life expectancy at birth will improve by 2.5 years for each five-year period until a life expectancy of 70 years has been reached. Beyond 70 years, the quinquennial improvement will be gradually reduced. A maximum male life expectancy of 72.6 years and a maximum female life expectancy of 75 years are assumed.[10]

Mortality in the Less Developed Countries

According to the United Nations, the average gain in life expectancies in the less developed countries will be 9 years over the course of the 20-year period 1970/1975–1995; that is, average life expectancies will increase from 52.2 to 60.7 years. The World Health Organization projects a comparable trend, with life expectancy at birth reaching 60 to 65 years by the year 2000.[11] If

[9]Here an alternative exists: The rate of decrease in mortality can be constant or decline over time, i.e., there can be an addition of two years to life expectancy every five years for any period considered or an increase every five years that becomes smaller and smaller as one approaches the end of the projection.

[10]UN, Department of Economic and Social Affairs, Population Division, *World Population Prospects as Assessed in 1973*, (ST/ESA/Ser.A60), pp. 11, 12.

[11]UN, World Health Organization, *Report of the Meeting on Programs of Analysis of Mortality Trends and Levels*, Geneva, June 1969 (E/CN.G/221), p. 692.

TABLE 2
Working Model for Projecting Mortality Levels in Terms of Life Expectancies at Birth for Both Sexes Aged 55 Years and Over

Time Reference (yr)	Males	Females	Both Sexes Combined
t*	53.50	56.50	55.00
t + 5	55.80	58.90	57.30
t + 10	58.05	61.20	59.60
t + 15	60.10	63.40	61.70
t + 20	62.00	65.50	63.70
t + 25	63.75	67.50	65.60
t + 30	65.35	69.40	67.30
t + 35	66.80	71.10	68.90
t + 40	68.10	72.60	70.30
t + 45	69.25	73.90	71.50
t + 50	70.25	75.00	72.60
t + 55	71.10	75.90	73.40
t + 60	71.75	76.60	74.10
t + 65	72.20	77.10	74.60
t + 70	72.45	77.40	74.90
t + 75	72.65	77.50	75.00

*The time reference t refers to the beginning year.
SOURCE: UN, Department of Economic and Social Affairs, Population Division, *World Population Prospects as Assessed in 1973*, (ST/ESA/Ser. A60), p. 11.

such an increase is attained, it will have significant implications for the countries involved. Are these projections too optimistic or too pessimistic? They are based on lessons drawn from the study of the past evolution of mortality in the developed countries, where three stages have been observed in the process of mortality reduction:

During the first phase, the situation with respect to mortality, which is very unfavorable at the beginning, improves slowly and irregularly. The second phase is characterized by a much stronger improvement, with mortality declining rapidly and regularly until it reaches a moderate level. Progress is again slower during the final phase, when efforts designed to reduce even further the already reduced mortality rates confront growing difficulties, until such a time when it is almost impossible to make additional improvements.[12]

At the present time, the less developed countries are not all in the same stage of this process. Certain ones seem to have already entered the third phase, some are in the intermediary phase of rapid growth, and others are still in the initial phase of high mortality. If one considers the less developed countries as a whole, it appears that the most rapid growth in life expectancy was achieved during the 1950s, and in the future one can expect growth to become much slower, although it will remain relatively high during the next two decades, which are of principal concern to us. For these countries, the future evolution of mortality will depend primarily, if not exclusively, on economic and social organization rather than on medical progress, to improve living conditions.[13] Therefore it is scarcely likely that the limit of 60 to 65 years in life expectancy projected by the UN and the World Health Organization can be increased.[14] It is doubtful that even this limit will be reached, for it was projected on the assumption that an economic take-off would occur, and this raises more general questions as to how development will proceed in these countries.

Mortality in the Developed Countries

For the developed countries, the UN foresees an increase in life expectancy at birth from 71.1 years in 1970–1975 to 73.0 in

[12]UN, Department of Economic and Social Affairs, Population Division, "Selected World Demographic Indicators by Countries, 1950–2000," May 28, 1975 (ESA/P/WP/55).

[13]UN, *Recent Population Trends and Future Prospects*, item 7 of Provisional Agenda, World Population Conference, Bucharest, 1974 (E/CONF60.3).

[14]See J. Vallin, "La Mortalité dans les Pays du Tiers Monde: Évolution and Perspectives," *Population*, no. 5, September–October 1968, pp. 845–868.

1990–1995, a total increase of less than 2 years. And even this rather modest improvement can perhaps be questioned if it is juxtaposed with the evolution of 1955–1969, during which period life expectancy scarcely changed and at times even fell, especially for males.[15] On the contrary, the World Health Organization estimates that a life expectancy on the order of 75 to 80 years can be attained by the end of the century.

What can be made of these divergent predictions? A comparison of previous forecasts and observed data leads to a cautious position. In these forecasts, the increase in life expectancy of women was slightly understimated, while that of men was notably overestimated. Rather than taking into account several changes in trends, previous projections suggested, quite wrongly, that the evolution of mortality was stable and that all one had to do was simply to extend past trends in order to move from diagnosis to forecast.

In support of either an optimistic or a pessimistic thesis, there are several arguments. Certainly the disparities in life expectancy that do exist between countries, between regions, within a single country, or between social groups and classes indicate that several years of life expectancy can still be added;[16] but under all hypotheses, given the present state of medical knowledge—in particular, knowledge about the process of aging—any gain must be strictly limited. Thus, "in the United States it has been calculated that the elimination of all deaths occurring before the age of 65 years would result in an increase in life expectancy at birth to 79 years."[17] It has also been calculated that "in France, eliminating all cancer deaths would only add 2.5 years to average life expectancy."[18]

To determine more precisely what are the limits to mortality

---

[15]The record for excessive male mortality belongs to the Soviet Union (with a gap of 10 years in average life expectancy between men and women).

[16]UN, *Recent Population Trends and Future Prospects*, Bucharest, 1974, (E/CONF60.3).

[17]Ibid.

[18]H. Le Bras and G. Tapinos, *Les Perspectives Démographiques à Long Terme et Leurs Conséquences: Communication au Colloque Franco-Sovietique sur les Méthodes de Planification et de Prévision à Long Terme*, working papers, Institut National d'Études Démographiques, Paris, October 1975.

reduction, it is useful to examine infant mortality and specific causes of adult mortality.

Infant mortality, whose spectacular reduction in modern times compared with earlier historical epochs has constituted the most important factor in the improvement in mortality in the developed countries, can be reduced still further. What suggests this is the fact that there are still differences among and within countries classified as developed, although if one excludes from this classification certain countries that really are relatively undeveloped, such as Albania, Portugal, and Yugoslavia, the differences are rather small. For the years 1965–1969, according to the World Health Organization, the infant mortality rate in the most advanced countries (Sweden, for example) was at 12 to 13 per thousand as opposed to 20 to 22 per thousand in some other highly developed countries (the United States, France, the Federal Republic of Germany, the German Democratic Republic); it stands at 86.7 per thousand in Albania, 62.5 per thousand in Portugal, and 62.1 per thousand in Yugoslavia. In 1971 the infant mortality rate fell to 11.1 per thousand in Sweden, 17.1 per thousand in France, and 19.1 per thousand in the United States.[19]

Detailed studies show that efforts to prevent infant deaths ought to be concentrated in the first days, even the first hours, after birth. According to the World Health Organization, "most infant deaths are attributable to immaturity (the primary factor being low birth weight), birth injury, or congenital malformation."[20] Moreover, greater attention to prenatal care would lead to the avoidance of certain high-risk births. According to the World Health Organization, an infant mortality rate on the order of 5 to 10 per thousand could be reached by the end of the century, and for certain countries this would translate into an increase of 2 years in life expectancy.

Also, a reduction of mortality in adults can be expected. According to the World Health Organization, the two principal

[19]See J. E. C. Weatherall, "Infant Mortality: International Differences," *Population Trends*, no. 1, Autumn 1975, pp. 9–12.

[20]UN Department of Economic and Social Affairs, Population Division, *Report of the Meeting on Programs of Analysis of Mortality*, May 28, 1975, (ESA/P/WP/55).

causes of death for individuals aged 15 to 44 are accidents and malignant tumors. For those aged 45 to 64, the major killers are heart attacks, lung cancer, other respiratory illnesses, and accidents. These causes pertain principally to men, whose death rate increases in the latter age group, whereas that of women tends to decline. According to the World Health Organization, it would be possible to eliminate half the deaths of men and one-quarter of the deaths of women aged 45 to 64 solely by taking action to improve living conditions and the environment.

Will death rates necessarily rise as industrialization proceeds? Malthus thought so, and industrialization has produced an increase in work-related accidents. The question, however, is more general. Do relatively developed societies create new causes of death, such as pollution and auto accidents? Or do such societies significantly increase the incidence of certain traditional causes of death, such as urban violence and suicide? The latter assertion is perhaps true to a certain degree, but the increased incidence is rather slight.

In any case, the future improvement of mortality in the developed countries, unlike that of the less developed ones, depends as much on medical progress as on general economic progress—if not more so. Nevertheless, it is important to distinguish between relevant advances that may occur in scientific knowledge and the probability of resources being allocated for the application and diffusion of such knowledge. The costs of medical techniques that can save the lives of seriously ill persons are skyrocketing, and these costs also increase the burden on a nation as a whole. As a demographer said realistically, it will become necessary to select those whom one is going to allow to die. Predicting mortality levels will thus be transformed into a normative question relating to political choices and the means of selecting among collective priorities.

We have so far reviewed mortality from a traditional medical point of view, leaving aside the genetic problem of longevity. There is general agreement that if all the causes of death except aging were eliminated, life expectancy would be about 110 years. In the period before modernization, average life expectancy at birth did not exceed 25 years, and in the countries that were the first to undergo the demographic revolution, life expectancy increased to 70 years in the space of only two centuries. This is a real revolution, and progress is still possible, as we have said, through improvements in medical and economic conditions. It will require another revolution to analyze and overcome the cellular process of aging. If such a revolution occurs, humanity will enter a new stage in the prolongation of life expectancy.

AN ALTERNATIVE METHODOLOGY

Demographic forecasting is essentially a statistical extrapolation of observed trends to which one adds low- and high-probability variants in order to ensure a safe margin of error. These forecasts originally focused on developments in the growth rates of the world's population as a whole, but projections of various population components—that is, different age cohorts, taking into account age-specific mortality and fertility rates—are now considered more significant.

Demographic projections have traditionally been accepted as fate, as an infrastructure to which everything else must adapt, as a master variable. This attitude is based on the assumption that since society is stable, trends from the past can be extrapolated into the future. And this was more or less the case in traditional societies, except for the wars and natural catastrophes that have always upset middle-term and long-term projections. But stability is no longer characteristic of contemporary societies, except in the short run, and it is the middle term and long term that are precisely the time frames of demographic projections. Thus the major difficulty in developing projections at the present time stems precisely from the fact that societies in the developed world, like those in the less developed world, are undergoing a profound transformation. Some are trying to cope with the costs of economic growth; others are trying to achieve a certain level of well-being, of which the ideal pattern is set by the developed countries.

Since demographic trends are one expression of the way society as a whole operates, the traditional logic of projections must be reversed. We should begin by trying to foresee the principal changes that a society will undergo during the course of the years to come in order to guess what modifications in behavior will result, and how these in turn will bear upon demographic trends.

Societies have many characteristic elements with very important demographic implications, and one of these is the recognized role of women. The social status of women is one of the essential factors that directly determine fertility levels. If in the future a higher proportion of women wish to have independent financial means and as a consequence enter into professional roles, there is no doubt that this will have a very clear effect in lowering fertility; we know that the number of working women is in part a function of the number of young children in households. The logic of projections must therefore be reversed: one should begin by trying to foresee the principal changes that a society will undergo during the course of the years to come in order to predict what modifications in behavior will result and then determine how these, in turn, will bear upon demographic trends, including fertility levels. This way of looking at things would permit a better understanding of, to cite just one example, the real obstacles, such as traditional marital practices in India and China, which at the present time prevent the diffusion of contraceptive practices in the less developed countries. In short, it is necessary, although difficult, to understand social life in its entirety in order to determine what Judith Blake calls "the social context of reproduction" and to deduce the demographic structures that are associated with it.[21] Projections of world population are thus filled with methodological pitfalls and uncertainties. But because population bears so importantly upon so many other issues, projections must be developed and everyone has to remain cautions about their use.

[21]Blake's study, *Family Structure in Jamaica: The Social Context of Reproduction*, The Free Press, Glencoe, Ill., and the classic work of Phillip Ariès, *Centuries of Childhood, A Social History of Family Life*, Random House, New York, 1965, are in their own ways examples of the methods that we have in mind.

Selected Bibliography

Brass, W.: "Perspectives in Population Predictions" (with discussion), *Journal of the Royal Statistical Society*, vol. 137, pt. 4, 1974, pp. 532–583.

Brown, Lester: *World Population Trends: Signs of Hope, Signs of Stress*, paper 8, Worldwatch Institute, Washington, D.C., October 1976.

Browning, L.: "Migrant Selectivity and the Growth of Large Cities in Developing Societies," in *Rapid Population Growth*, vol. 2, Johns Hopkins University Press for the National Academy of Sciences, Baltimore, 1971, pp. 273–314.

Chen, Pi-chao: *Population and Health Policy in the People's Republic of China*, Occasional Monograph Series No. 9, Smithsonian Institution Interdisciplinary Communications Program, Washington, D.C., December 1976.

Coale, Ansley: "The Demographic Transition Reconsidered," in *International Population Conference, Liège, 1973*, International Union for the Scientific Study of Population, Liège, Belgium, vol. 1, 1974.

————, and Edgar M. Hoover: *Population Growth and Economic Development in Low-Income Countries: A Case Study of India's Prospects*, Princeton University Press, Princeton, 1958.

Dorn, F.: "Pitfalls in Population Forecasts and Projections," *Journal of the American Statistical Association*, September 1950.

Freedman, Ronald, and Bernard Berelson: "The Record of Family Planning Programs," *Studies in Family Planning*, Population Council, New York, January 1976, pp. 1–40.

Frejka, Tomas: *The Future of Population Growth: Alternative Paths to Equilibrium*, John Wiley & Sons, New York, 1973.

————: *Reference Tables to "The Future of Population Growth."* Population Council, New York, 1973.

Habakkuk, H. J.: *Population Growth and Economic Development Since 1750*, Leicester University Press, Leicester, England, 1971.

Kahn, H., and B. Bruce-Briggs: *Things to Come: Thinking About the Seventies and Eighties*, The Macmillan Co., New York, 1972.

Keyfitz, Nathan: "On Future Population," *Journal of the American Statistical Society*, July 1972, pp. 347–363.

McGreevey, William P.: *The Policy Relevance of Recent Social Research on Fertility*, Occasional Monograph Series No. 2, Smithsonian Institution, Washington, D.C., September 1974.

McNamara, Robert S.: "Address to the Massachusetts Institute of Technology," The MIT Press, Cambridge, Mass., April 28, 1977.

Mauldin, W. Parker, et al.: "A Report on Bucharest," *Studies in Family Planning*, vol. 5, no. 12, Population Council, New York, December 1975, pp. 357–395.

Meadows, D. L., et al.: *The Dynamics of Growth in a Finite World*, Wright Allen Press, Cambridge, Mass., 1974.

Moore-Cavar, Emily Campbell: *International Inventory of Information on Induced Abortion*, Columbia University Press for the International Institute for the Study of Human Reproduction, New York, 1974, pp. 76–88.

Nortman, Dorothy: "Changing Contraceptive Patterns: A Global Perspective," *Population Bulletin*, vol. 32, no. 3, Population Reference Bureau, Washington, D.C., August 1977.

————: "Population and Family Planning Programs: A Factbook," *Reports on Population/Family Planning*, no. 2, 8th ed., Population Council, New York, October 1976, pp. 3–16.

Rock, John: *The Time Has Come: A Catholic Doctor's Proposals to End the Battle over Birth Control*, Alfred A. Knopf, New York, 1963.

Salas, Rafael: *People: An International Choice*, Pergamon Press, New York, 1976.

Shyrock, J. S., J. S. Siegel, et al.: *The Methods and Materials of Demography*, 2 vols., U.S. Department of Commerce, Bureau of the Census, Washington, D.C., May 1973.

Stokes, Bruce: *Filling the Family Planning Gap*, paper 12, Worldwatch Institute, Washington, D.C., May 1977, pp. 1–8.

Teitelbaum, M. S.: "The Relevance of Demographic Transition: A Theory for Developing Countries," *Science*, vol. 188, no. 4186, May 2, 1975, pp. 420–425.

United Nations, Department of Economic and Social Affairs, *The Determinants and Consequences of Population Trends*, New York, 1973 (ST/SOA/Ser. A/50), vol. 1. For additional UN publications, see list below.

U.S. Bureau of the Census: *The Two-Child Family and Population Growth: An International View*, Washington, D.C., 1971.

Vumbaco, Brenda: "Recent Law and Policy Changes in Fertility Control," *Population Reports*, series E, no. 4, Population Information Program, Washington, D.C., March 1976, pp. E41–E52.

Zachariah, K. C., and R. Cuca: *Population Projections for Bank Member Countries, 1970–2000*, World Bank, Population and Human Resources Division, Washington, D.C., 1972.

UN PUBLICATIONS

Center for Economic and Social Information

"World Population Plan of Action" (reprint of conference text), *Action Taken at Bucharest*, 1974.

Department of Economic and Social Affairs, Population Division

1. Review of Projections Made before 1968
   "The Past and Future Growth of World Population—A Long-Range View," *Population Bulletin No. 1* (sales no. 52.XIII.2).

   "Framework for Future Population Estimates, 1950–1980, by World Regions," *Proceedings of the World Population Conference*, Rome, 1954, vol. 3 (sales no. 55.XIII.8), pp. 283–328.

   The Future Growth of World Population (sales no. 58.XIII.2).

   World Population Prospects as Assessed in 1963 (sales no. 66.XIII.2).

2. 1968 Series and Corrections Made for the Bucharest Conference
   "Recent Population Trends and Future Prospects" (Item 7 of the Provisional Agenda) (E/CONF60.3).

"World and Regional Population Prospects," April 16, 1974 (E/CONF/ 60/CBP/15).

"World Comprehensive Demographic Projections, 1965–1985," June 1974 (ESA/P/WP/52).

World Population Prospects as Assessed in 1968 (sales no. 72.XIII.4).

3. 1973 Series
World Population Prospects as Assessed in 1973 (ST/ESA/Ser. A60).

"Trends and Prospects in Urban and Rural Population, 1950–2000, as Assessed in 1973–1974" (ESA/P/WP/54).

"Selected World Demographic Indicators by Countries, 1950–2000," May 28, 1975 (ESA/P/WP/55).

"Trends and Prospects in the Populations of Urban Agglomerations, 1950–2000, as Assessed in 1973–1975," November 21, 1975 (ESA/P/WP58).

4. "World Population Prospects as Assessed in 1973," 1977 (ST/ESA/SER.A/ 60).

FAO

"Population, Food Supply, and Agricultural Development," June 4, 1974 (E/CONF60/CBP/25).

ILO

"The Labor Force and World Population Growth," *Bulletin of Labor Statistics*, special edition, 1974.

Todaro, Michael P.: *Internal Migration in Developing Countries*, 1976.

"World and Regional Labor Force Prospects to the Year 2000," May 29, 1974 (E/CONF60/CBP/31).

UNESCO

"Educational Development: World and Regional Statistics, Trends, and Projections until 1985," April 10, 1974 (E/CONF60/BP/10).

Appendix

APPENDIX TABLE 1

Projected Total Population by Region and Country, 1970–2000, UN Medium Variant

Region and Country	Population (thousands)						
	1970	1975	1980	1985	1990	1995	2000
World total	3,610,377	3,967,864	4,374,110	4,816,537	5,280,017	5,762,564	6,254,377
More developed regions	1,084,018	1,131,684	1,181,002	1,230,706	1,277,396	1,319,849	1,360,245
Less developed regions	2,526,359	2,836,180	3,193,108	3,585,832	4,002,621	4,442,714	4,894,133
Africa	351,727	401,314	460,915	531,701	614,085	708,453	813,681
Eastern Africa	99,818	114,498	131,992	152,868	177,581	206,659	239,861
British Indian Ocean Territory	2	2	2	2	2	2	2
Burundi	3,350	3,765	4,288	4,904	5,618	6,417	7,280
Comoros	270	306	347	391	428	454	475
Ethiopia	24,855	27,975	31,522	35,739	40,708	46,673	53,665
French Territory of the Afars and the Issas	95	106	119	135	152	169	187
Kenya	11,247	13,251	15,688	18,605	22,102	26,263	31,020
Madagascar	6,932	8,020	9,329	10,909	12,800	15,079	17,782
Malawi	4,360	4,916	5,577	6,369	7,306	8,360	9,540
Mauritius[a]	824	899	969	1,039	1,113	1,188	1,257
Mozambique	8,234	9,239	10,375	11,747	13,401	15,375	17,649
Reunion	447	501	548	594	639	686	732
Rwanda	3,679	4,200	4,865	5,654	6,568	7,607	8,707
Seychelles	52	59	66	74	83	92	102
Somalia	2,789	3,170	3,652	4,236	4,907	5,679	6,544
Southern Rhodesia	5,308	6,276	7,495	8,985	10,757	12,815	15,147
Uganda	9,806	11,353	13,222	15,423	17,996	20,932	24,160
United Republic of Tanzania	13,273	15,438	18,052	21,142	24,805	29,130	34,045
Zambia	4,295	5,022	5,875	6,919	8,195	9,739	11,566

Middle Africa	40,446	45,310	51,201	58,356	66,735	76,485	87,732
Angola	5,670	6,353	7,181	8,188	9,385	10,808	12,462
Central African Republic	1,612	1,790	2,004	2,276	2,590	2,949	3,360
Chad	3,640	4,023	4,473	4,978	5,546	6,187	6,912
Congo	1,191	1,345	1,532	1,762	2,032	2,349	2,720
Equatorial Guinea	285	310	339	372	410	452	497
Gabon	500	526	546	568	593	625	660
Sao Tome and Principe	74	80	85	87	88	88	88
United Republic of Cameroon	5,836	6,398	7,088	7,987	9,030	10,218	11,583
Zaire	21,638	24,485	27,952	32,139	37,061	42,809	49,450
Northern Africa	85,627	98,185	113,055	130,334	149,748	170,525	191,824
Algeria	14,330	16,792	19,828	23,501	27,741	32,226	36,663
Egypt	33,329	37,543	42,144	47,191	52,640	58,438	64,588
Libyan Arab Republic	1,938	2,255	2,638	3,086	3,590	4,144	4,737
Morocco	15,126	17,504	20,384	23,788	27,633	31,752	35,904
Sudan	15,695	18,268	21,420	25,147	29,425	34,123	38,977
Tunisia	5,137	5,747	6,561	7,537	8,629	9,748	10,853
Western Sahara [b]	72	75	79	84	89	95	101
Southern Africa	24,335	27,853	32,179	37,143	42,692	49,050	56,231
Botswana	617	691	795	923	1,072	1,240	1,429
Lesotho	1,043	1,148	1,284	1,440	1,617	1,813	2,027
Namibia	766	883	1,024	1,192	1,390	1,621	1,883
South Africa	21,500	24,663	28,533	32,955	37,881	43,539	49,951
Swaziland	409	468	543	633	732	838	941
Western Africa	101,501	115,469	132,488	153,000	177,329	205,734	238,034
Benin	2,686	3,074	3,534	4,070	4,681	5,324	5,921
Cape Verde	268	295	323	351	379	406	432

[a] Including Agalega, Rodrigues, and St. Brandon.
[b] Formerly referred to as Spanish Sahara.

189

APPENDIX TABLE 1 (Continued)
Projected Total Population by Region and Country, 1970–2000, UN Medium Variant

Region and Country	Population (thousands)						
	1970	1975	1980	1985	1990	1995	2000
Western Africa (cont'd.)							
Gambia	463	509	563	624	694	772	852
Ghana	8,628	9,873	11,446	13,395	15,710	18,355	21,164
Guinea	3,921	4,416	5,014	5,718	6,538	7,454	8,455
Guinea-Bissau	487	525	573	631	695	767	842
Ivory Coast	4,310	4,885	5,579	6,399	7,358	8,435	9,617
Liberia	1,523	1,708	1,937	2,199	2,500	2,843	3,219
Mali	5,047	5,697	6,470	7,374	8,455	9,746	11,257
Mauritania	1,162	1,283	1,427	1,596	1,795	2,025	2,281
Niger	4,016	4,592	5,272	6,077	7,049	8,212	9,568
Nigeria	55,073	62,925	72,596	84,400	98,497	115,258	134,924
Senegal	3,925	4,418	4,989	5,642	6,408	7,262	8,171
St. Helena[c]	5	5	5	6	6	6	6
Sierra Leone	2,644	2,983	3,392	3,870	4,419	5,043	5,716
Togo	1,960	2,248	2,596	3,008	3,494	4,050	4,640
Upper Volta	5,384	6,032	6,774	7,639	8,651	9,776	10,969
Latin America	283,020	324,092	371,631	425,635	485,585	550,603	619,929
Caribbean	24,616	27,116	30,016	33,272	36,847	40,662	44,504
Antigua	70	73	75	78	80	83	85
Bahamas	177	204	230	255	280	304	330
Barbados	239	245	252	259	269	278	285
British Virgin I.	10	11	13	15	16	18	19
Cayman I.	11	11	12	12	12	13	13

Cuba	8,565	9,481	10,533	11,660	12,855	14,069	15,267
Dominica	71	75	80	85	88	90	91
Dominican Republic	4,343	5,118	6,052	7,171	8,492	10,022	11,762
Grenada	94	96	98	100	102	104	106
Guadeloupe	328	354	382	412	440	467	493
Haiti	4,235	4,552	4,956	5,441	5,980	6,558	7,045
Jamaica	1,882	2,029	2,172	2,316	2,464	2,609	2,726
Martinique	338	363	391	419	443	465	485
Montserrat	12	13	13	13	14	14	14
Netherlands Antilles	222	242	267	298	331	363	389
Puerto Rico	2,743	2,902	3,075	3,257	3,431	3,587	3,723
St. Kitts–Nevis–Anguilla	65	66	67	67	68	69	70
St. Lucia	101	108	115	122	127	130	130
St. Vincent	88	93	98	102	106	108	109
Trinidad & Tobago	955	1,009	1,062	1,116	1,172	1,230	1,280
Turks and Caicos I.	6	6	6	6	6	6	6
U.S. Virgin I.	63	66	68	70	73	74	76
Middle America	67,003	78,652	92,631	109,180	128,160	149,315	172,670
Belize	120	140	162	184	205	223	234
Costa Rica	1,737	1,994	2,286	2,611	2,954	3,311	3,695
El Salvador	3,516	4,108	4,813	5,643	6,595	7,654	8,803
Guatemala	5,298	6,129	7,100	8,210	9,460	10,849	12,374
Honduras	2,553	3,037	3,595	4,241	4,997	5,875	6,881
Mexico	50,313	59,204	69,965	82,803	97,585	114,055	132,244
Nicaragua	1,970	2,318	2,733	3,218	3,778	4,422	5,154
Panama[d]	1,458	1,678	1,930	2,217	2,533	2,871	3,230
Canal Zone	39	43	47	52	53	54	55

[c]Including Ascension and Tristan da Cunha.
[d]Excluding Panama Canal Zone.

191

APPENDIX TABLE 1 (Continued)

Projected Total Population by Region and Country, 1970–2000, UN Medium Variant

Region and Country	Population (thousands)						
	1970	1975	1980	1985	1990	1995	2000
Temperate South America							
Argentina	36,073	38,747	41,564	44,407	47,152	49,719	52,078
Chile	23,748	25,384	27,064	28,678	30,189	31,584	32,861
Falkland I. (Malvinas)	9,369	10,253	11,235	12,303	13,379	14,405	15,355
Uruguay	2	2	2	2	2	2	2
	2,955	3,108	3,263	3,425	3,582	3,729	3,861
Tropical South America	155,328	179,578	207,421	238,774	273,426	310,907	350,676
Bolivia	4,780	5,410	6,162	7,013	7,974	9,054	10,267
Brazil	95,204	109,730	126,389	145,082	165,757	188,273	212,507
Colombia	22,075	25,890	30,215	35,050	40,324	45,874	51,464
Ecuador	6,031	7,090	8,303	9,689	11,251	12,962	14,773
French Guiana	51	60	71	82	94	106	118
Guyana	709	791	884	984	1,080	1,172	1,256
Paraguay	2,301	2,647	3,062	3,540	4,074	4,655	5,274
Peru	13,248	15,326	17,711	20,424	23,478	26,871	30,561
Surinam	371	422	491	584	688	797	904
Venezuela	10,559	12,213	14,134	16,326	18,706	21,143	23,552
Northern America	226,389	236,841	248,833	262,344	275,136	286,163	296,199
Bermuda	52	56	60	64	68	72	76
Canada	21,406	22,801	24,576	26,511	28,357	30,000	31,613
Greenland	47	54	59	63	67	71	75
St. Pierre & Miquelon	5	5	5	5	5	5	5
U.S.A.	204,879	213,925	224,133	235,701	246,639	256,015	264,430

East Asia	926,866	1,006,380	1,087,749	1,164,848	1,233,498	1,301,942	1,370,061
China	771,840	838,803	907,609	973,155	1,031,142	1,089,572	1,147,987
Japan	104,331	111,120	117,546	122,445	126,213	129,567	132,929
Other East Asia	50,694	56,456	62,594	69,247	76,143	82,803	89,145
Democratic People's Republic of Korea	13,892	15,852	17,926	20,179	22,581	25,022	27,457
Hong Kong	3,942	4,225	4,522	4,841	5,147	5,405	5,625
Macau	248	271	292	314	334	353	372
Mongolia	1,248	1,446	1,669	1,914	2,176	2,441	2,701
Republic of Korea	31,365	34,663	38,185	42,000	45,905	49,583	52,991
South Asia	1,101,199	1,249,793	1,426,843	1,624,722	1,836,258	2,053,610	2,267,266
Eastern South Asia	282,969	323,836	370,855	423,221	478,712	535,640	591,622
Brunei	133	147	160	175	189	202	216
Burma	27,748	31,240	35,195	39,687	44,573	49,701	54,902
Democratic Kampuchea	7,060	8,110	9,409	10,911	12,491	14,139	15,819
East Timor	604	672	755	846	943	1,044	1,145
Indonesia[e]	119,467	136,044	154,869	175,471	196,576	217,623	237,507
Lao People's Democratic Republic	2,962	3,303	3,721	4,182	4,678	5,199	5,725
Malaysia	10,466	12,093	13,998	16,076	18,260	20,239	22,054
Philippines	37,604	44,437	52,203	60,842	70,119	79,876	89,707
Singapore	2,075	2,248	2,437	2,636	2,829	2,993	3,126
Socialist Republic of Vietnam	39,106	43,451	48,634	54,612	61,302	68,491	75,802
Former Democratic Republic of Vietnam	21,154	23,798	26,901	30,455	34,431	38,729	43,141
Former Republic of South Vietnam	17,952	19,653	21,733	24,157	26,871	29,762	32,661
Thailand	35,745	42,093	49,473	57,784	66,752	76,135	85,618
Middle South Asia	741,710	837,799	953,997	1,083,462	1,221,669	1,362,961	1,501,213
Afghanistan	16,978	19,280	22,038	25,207	28,739	32,598	36,654
Bangladesh	67,692	73,746	84,803	98,003	112,694	128,298	144,347

eIncluding West Irian.

APPENDIX TABLE 1 (Continued)
Projected Total Population by Region and Country, 1970–2000, UN Medium Variant

Region and Country	Population (thousands)						
	1970	1975	1980	1985	1990	1995	2000
Middle South Asia (cont'd.)							
Bhutan	1,045	1,173	1,327	1,505	1,701	1,921	2,145
India	543,132	613,217	694,309	782,890	876,051	969,748	1,059,429
Iran	28,359	32,923	38,492	44,904	51,897	59,221	66,593
Maldives	108	119	132	147	165	184	205
Nepal	11,232	12,572	14,231	16,186	18,348	20,771	23,196
Pakistan	60,449	70,560	82,952	97,354	113,239	129,877	146,924
Sikkim	201	222	246	274	305	341	381
Sri Lanka	12,514	13,986	15,465	16,992	18,530	20,002	21,339
Western South Asia	76,520	88,158	101,992	118,039	135,877	155,009	174,432
Bahrain	215	251	294	344	403	468	536
Cyprus	633	673	714	755	791	821	846
Democratic Yemen	1,436	1,660	1,928	2,241	2,601	3,002	3,425
Gaza Strip[f] (Palestine[g])	501	594	707	843	999	1,166	1,348
Iraq	9,356	11,067	13,145	15,578	18,277	21,242	24,445
Israel	2,958	3,317	3,898	4,364	4,791	5,186	5,566
Jordan	2,280	2,688	3,177	3,752	4,397	5,114	5,889
Kuwait	760	1,085	1,439	1,816	2,229	2,690	3,183
Lebanon	2,469	2,869	3,360	3,956	4,637	5,373	6,118
Oman	657	766	898	1,053	1,231	1,429	1,639
Qatar	79	92	108	127	148	172	197
Saudi Arabia	7,740	8,966	10,423	12,132	14,094	16,285	18,600
Syrian Arab Republic	6,247	7,259	8,536	10,081	11,823	13,750	15,824

Turkey	35,232	39,882	45,363	51,692	58,656	65,843	72,588
United Arab Emirates	190	222	260	304	356	413	474
Yemen	5,767	6,668	7,741	9,000	10,445	12,054	13,753
Europe	459,085	473,098	486,541	499,972	513,605	526,755	539,500
Eastern Europe	102,942	106,267	109,647	112,771	115,607	118,405	121,437
Bulgaria	8,490	8,793	9,075	9,323	9,554	9,789	10,036
Czechoslovakia	14,339	14,793	15,250	15,646	15,996	16,356	16,796
German Democratic Republic[h]	17,058	17,127	17,228	17,368	17,532	17,710	17,932
Hungary	10,338	10,534	10,721	10,841	10,907	10,972	11,069
Poland	32,473	33,841	35,316	36,685	37,824	38,822	39,846
Romania	20,244	21,178	22,057	22,908	23,793	24,755	25,758
Northern Europe	80,309	81,975	83,740	85,501	87,424	89,355	91,320
Channel I.	122	128	133	138	143	147	152
Denmark	4,929	5,026	5,104	5,172	5,238	5,303	5,361
Faeroe I.	39	40	41	43	44	45	47
Finland	4,606	4,652	4,688	4,708	4,734	4,744	4,747
Iceland	204	216	229	243	256	267	278
Ireland	2,954	3,131	3,298	3,476	3,658	3,834	4,002
Isle of Man	56	58	60	63	65	66	68
Norway	3,877	4,007	4,121	4,222	4,314	4,400	4,483
Sweden	8,043	8,291	8,546	8,770	8,981	9,184	9,390
U.K.	55,480	56,427	57,519	58,667	59,993	61,363	62,794

[f] Comprising that part of Palestine under Egyptian administration following the Armistice of 1949 until June 1967, when it was occupied by Israeli military forces.

[g] Former mandated territory administered by the United Kingdom until the Armistice of 1949.

[h] Including Berlin. Designations and data for Berlin appearing on these pages were supplied by the competent authorities pursuant to the relevant agreements of the Four Powers.

APPENDIX TABLE 1 (Continued)
Projected Total Population by Region and Country, 1970–2000, UN Medium Variant

Region and Country	Population (thousands)						
	1970	1975	1980	1985	1990	1995	2000
Southern Europe	127,696	132,354	137,106	141,875	146,669	151,293	155,685
Andorra	19	23	25	28	31	34	37
Albania	2,169	2,482	2,831	3,207	3,584	3,934	4,263
Gibraltar	26	27	28	29	30	31	31
Greece	8,793	8,930	9,080	9,223	9,369	9,506	9,621
Holy See	1	1	1	1	1	1	1
Italy	53,565	55,023	56,319	57,508	58,677	59,801	60,876
Malta	326	329	335	340	341	340	336
Portugal	8,628	8,762	8,957	9,201	9,463	9,707	9,918
San Marino	19	20	21	22	23	24	25
Spain	33,779	35,433	37,209	39,080	41,041	43,008	44,924
Yugoslavia	20,371	21,322	22,299	23,236	24,107	24,908	25,653
Western Europe	148,137	152,503	156,049	159,825	163,906	167,702	171,058
Austria	7,447	7,538	7,628	7,733	7,856	7,985	8,118
Belgium	9,638	9,846	10,061	10,273	10,464	10,625	10,781
France	50,670	52,913	55,103	57,052	58,816	60,508	62,131
Germany, Federal Republic of[h]	60,700	61,682	62,023	62,858	64,188	65,370	66,242
Liechtenstein	21	22	23	24	25	27	28
Luxembourg	339	342	345	347	350	352	353
Monaco	23	24	25	26	27	28	28
Netherlands	13,032	13,599	14,107	14,614	15,116	15,588	16,010
Switzerland	6,267	6,535	6,734	6,898	7,063	7,219	7,366
Oceania	19,323	21,308	23,482	25,777	28,109	30,431	32,715

Australia and New Zealand	15,371	16,840	18,403	19,997	21,549	23,038	24,512
Australia	12,552	13,809	15,140	16,490	17,796	19,034	20,245
New Zealand	2,820	3,031	3,263	3,507	3,753	4,004	4,267
Melanesia	2,771	3,126	3,555	4,057	4,630	5,246	5,847
New Caledonia	109	125	144	167	192	219	247
New Hebrides	84	96	111	129	148	169	190
Norfolk I.	2	2	2	2	2	2	2
Papua New Guinea	2,413	2,716	3,082	3,510	4,001	4,528	5,039
Solomon I.	163	187	216	250	287	328	369
Micronesia and Polynesia	1,181	1,341	1,524	1,722	1,930	2,147	2,356
Micronesia	267	306	350	398	448	502	556
Gilbert I. & Tuvalu	56	66	77	87	99	111	123
Guam	88	99	113	130	147	165	184
Nauru	7	8	8	9	9	10	10
Niue I.	5	5	6	6	7	7	7
Pacific I.	101	117	135	155	175	196	218
Other Micronesia^i	10	10	11	12	13	14	15
Polynesia	914	1,036	1,174	1,324	1,482	1,645	1,800
American Samoa	27	32	38	44	52	60	67
Cook I.	21	25	29	34	40	46	52
Fiji	520	577	635	691	745	798	847
French Polynesia	109	128	151	177	207	238	269
Tonga	86	101	119	140	163	188	212
Wallis & Futuna I.	9	9	9	9	9	9	9
Western Samoa	141	164	194	228	266	306	345
U.S.S.R.	242,768	255,038	268,115	281,540	293,742	304,607	315,027

^iIncluding Canton and Enderbury Islands, Christmas Island, Cocos (Keeling) Islands, Johnston Island, Midway Islands, Pitcairn Island, Tokelau Islands, and Wake Island.

SOURCE: UN, *World Population Prospects as Assessed in 1973*, pp. 90–97.

197

APPENDIX TABLE 2

Projected Average Annual Rates of Growth by Region and Country, 1970–2000, UN Medium Variant

Region and Country	Percentage					
	1970–1975	1975–1980	1980–1985	1985–1990	1990–1995	1995–2000
World total	1.89	1.95	1.93	1.84	1.75	1.64
More developed regions	0.86	0.85	0.82	0.74	0.65	0.60
Less developed regions	2.31	2.37	2.32	2.20	2.09	1.94
Africa	2.64	2.77	2.86	2.88	2.86	2.77
Eastern Africa	2.74	2.84	2.94	3.00	3.03	2.98
British Indian Ocean Territory	0.00	0.00	0.00	0.00	0.00	0.00
Burundi	2.33	2.60	2.69	2.72	2.66	2.52
Comoros	2.50	2.51	2.39	1.80	1.18	0.94
Ethiopia	2.36	2.39	2.51	2.60	2.73	2.79
French Territory of the Afars and the Issas	2.19	2.31	2.52	2.37	2.12	2.02
Kenya	3.28	3.38	3.41	3.45	3.45	3.33
Madagascar	2.92	3.02	3.13	3.20	3.28	3.30
Malawi	2.40	2.52	2.65	2.74	2.69	2.64
Mauritius[a]	1.76	1.49	1.39	1.38	1.30	1.13
Mozambique	2.30	2.32	2.48	2.64	2.75	2.76
Réunion	2.27	1.80	1.60	1.47	1.42	1.29
Rwanda	2.65	2.94	3.01	3.00	2.94	2.70
Seychelles	2.53	2.24	2.29	2.30	2.06	2.06
Somalia	2.56	2.83	2.97	2.94	2.92	2.84
Southern Rhodesia	3.35	3.55	3.63	3.60	3.50	3.34
Uganda	2.93	3.05	3.08	3.09	3.02	2.87
United Republic of Tanzania	3.02	3.13	3.16	3.20	3.21	3.12
Zambia	3.13	3.14	3.27	3.38	3.45	3.44

Middle Africa	2.27	2.44	2.62	2.68	2.73	2.74
Angola	2.27	2.45	2.62	2.73	2.82	2.85
Central African Republic	2.09	2.27	2.54	2.59	2.60	2.60
Chad	2.00	2.12	2.14	2.16	2.19	2.22
Congo	2.44	2.60	2.80	2.84	2.90	2.93
Equatorial Guinea	1.71	1.76	1.86	1.96	1.95	1.88
Gabon	1.00	0.76	0.77	0.90	1.03	1.10
Sao Tome and Principe	1.56	1.21	0.47	0.23	0.00	0.00
United Republic of Cameroon	1.84	2.05	2.39	2.45	2.47	2.51
Zaire	2.47	2.65	2.79	2.85	2.88	2.88
Northern Africa	2.74	2.82	2.84	2.78	2.60	2.35
Algeria	3.17	3.32	3.40	3.32	3.00	2.58
Egypt	2.38	2.31	2.26	2.19	2.09	2.00
Libyan Arab Republic	3.03	3.14	3.14	3.03	2.87	2.67
Morocco	2.92	3.05	3.09	3.00	2.78	2.46
Sudan	3.04	3.18	3.21	3.14	2.96	2.66
Tunisia	2.25	2.65	2.77	2.71	2.44	2.15
Western Sahara[b]	0.90	1.01	1.11	1.27	1.30	1.20
Southern Africa	2.70	2.89	2.87	2.78	2.78	2.73
Botswana	2.27	2.79	2.99	2.99	2.91	2.84
Lesotho	1.92	2.23	2.29	2.32	2.29	2.23
Namibia	2.84	2.98	3.03	3.07	3.07	3.00
South Africa	2.74	2.92	2.88	2.79	2.78	2.75
Swaziland	2.73	2.98	3.05	2.92	2.70	2.31
Western Africa	2.58	2.75	2.88	2.95	2.97	2.92
Benin	2.70	2.79	2.83	2.80	2.57	2.13
Cape Verde	1.91	1.79	1.67	1.55	1.38	1.24

[a]Including Agalega, Rodrigues, and St. Brandon.
[b]Formerly referred to as Spanish Sahara.

APPENDIX TABLE 2 (Continued)
Projected Average Annual Rates of Growth by Region and Country, 1970–2000, UN Medium Variant

Region and Country	Percentage					
	1970–1975	1975–1980	1980–1985	1985–1990	1990–1995	1995–2000
Western Africa (cont'd.)						
Gambia	1.92	2.01	2.04	2.13	2.12	1.98
Ghana	2.70	2.96	3.14	3.19	3.11	2.85
Guinea	2.38	2.54	2.63	2.68	2.62	2.52
Guinea–Bissau	1.51	1.76	1.92	1.94	1.96	1.87
Ivory Coast	2.51	2.66	2.74	2.79	2.73	2.62
Liberia	2.29	2.52	2.54	2.57	2.57	2.48
Mali	2.42	2.54	2.62	2.74	2.84	2.88
Mauritania	1.99	2.13	2.24	2.35	2.41	2.38
Niger	2.68	2.76	2.84	2.97	3.06	3.06
Nigeria	2.67	2.86	3.01	3.09	3.14	3.15
Senegal	2.37	2.43	2.46	2.55	2.50	2.36
St. Helena^c	0.78	0.75	0.73	0.70	0.68	0.66
Sierra Leone	2.41	2.57	2.64	2.65	2.64	2.51
Togo	2.74	2.88	2.95	2.99	2.96	2.72
Upper Volta	2.27	2.32	2.40	2.49	2.45	2.30
Latin America	2.71	2.74	2.71	2.64	2.51	2.37
Caribbean	1.93	2.03	2.06	2.04	1.97	1.81
Antigua	0.76	0.68	0.66	0.63	0.62	0.60
Bahamas	2.79	2.40	2.11	1.83	1.70	1.64
Barbados	0.50	0.58	0.53	0.76	0.63	0.51
British Virgin I.	3.47	2.80	2.32	2.08	1.77	1.63
Cayman I.	0.73	0.70	0.68	0.66	0.48	0.47

Cuba	2.03	2.10	2.03	1.95	1.81	1.63
Dominica	1.07	1.37	1.17	0.83	0.45	0.15
Dominican Republic	3.28	3.35	3.39	3.38	3.31	3.20
Grenada	0.42	0.41	0.40	0.40	0.39	0.38
Guadeloupe	1.55	1.51	1.49	1.32	1.22	1.08
Haiti	1.45	1.70	1.86	1.89	1.85	1.43
Jamaica	1.50	1.37	1.28	1.24	1.14	0.88
Martinique	1.44	1.44	1.40	1.12	0.96	0.84
Montserrat	0.65	0.63	0.61	0.59	0.43	0.42
Netherlands Antilles	1.71	1.96	2.20	2.12	1.87	1.38
Puerto Rico	1.13	1.16	1.15	1.04	0.89	0.74
St. Kitts–Nevis–Anguilla	0.28	0.27	0.27	0.27	0.23	0.26
St. Lucia	1.37	1.21	1.11	0.76	0.48	0.12
St. Vincent	1.22	1.01	0.88	0.65	0.45	0.22
Trinidad & Tobago	1.09	1.03	1.00	0.97	0.97	0.79
Turks and Caicos I.	0.00	0.00	0.00	0.00	0.00	0.00
United States Virgin I.	0.93	0.75	0.61	0.59	0.41	0.40
Middle America	3.21	3.27	3.29	3.21	3.06	2.91
Belize	3.11	2.90	2.53	2.17	1.69	0.95
Costa Rica	2.76	2.73	2.66	2.47	2.28	2.20
El Salvador	3.11	3.16	3.18	3.12	2.98	2.80
Guatemala	2.92	2.94	2.91	2.83	2.74	2.63
Honduras	3.48	3.37	3.31	3.28	3.24	3.16
Mexico	3.25	3.34	3.37	3.29	3.12	2.96
Nicaragua	3.26	3.29	3.27	3.21	3.15	3.06
Panama[d]	2.80	2.80	2.77	2.66	2.51	2.35
Canal Zone	1.99	1.81	1.97	0.38	0.41	0.33

[c]Including Ascension and Tristan da Cunha.
[d]Excluding Panama Canal Zone.

APPENDIX TABLE 2 (Continued)

Projected Average Annual Rates of Growth by Region and Country, 1970–2000, UN Medium Variant

Region and Country	Percentage					
	1970–1975	1975–1980	1980–1985	1985–1990	1990–1995	1995–2000
Temperate South America						
Argentina	1.43	1.40	1.32	1.20	1.06	0.93
Chile	1.33	1.28	1.16	1.03	0.90	0.79
Falkland I. (Malvinas)	1.80	1.83	1.82	1.68	1.48	1.28
Uruguay	0.00	0.00	0.00	0.00	0.00	0.00
	1.01	0.97	0.97	0.90	0.80	0.69
Tropical South America						
Bolivia	2.90	2.88	2.82	2.71	2.57	2.41
Brazil	2.48	2.60	2.59	2.57	2.54	2.51
Colombia	2.84	2.83	2.76	2.66	2.55	2.42
Ecuador	3.19	3.09	2.97	2.80	2.58	2.30
French Guiana	3.24	3.16	3.09	2.99	2.83	2.61
Guyana	3.51	3.27	3.01	2.70	2.41	2.10
Paraguay	2.17	2.22	2.14	1.86	1.64	1.39
Peru	2.80	2.91	2.90	2.81	2.67	2.50
Surinam	2.91	2.89	2.85	2.79	2.70	2.57
Venezuela	2.57	3.05	3.45	3.31	2.93	2.51
	2.91	2.92	2.88	2.72	2.45	2.16
Northern America						
Bermuda	0.90	0.99	1.06	0.95	0.79	0.69
Canada	1.47	1.37	1.25	1.18	1.14	1.11
Greenland	1.26	1.50	1.52	1.35	1.13	1.05
St. Pierre and Miquelon	2.80	1.78	1.32	1.24	1.17	1.08
United States of America	0.00	0.00	0.00	0.00	0.00	0.00
	0.86	0.93	1.01	0.91	0.75	0.65

East Asia	1.65	1.56	1.37	1.15	1.08	1.02
China	1.66	1.58	1.39	1.16	1.10	1.04
Japan	1.26	1.12	0.82	0.61	0.52	0.51
Other East Asia	2.15	2.06	2.02	1.90	1.68	1.48
Democratic People's Republic of Korea	2.64	2.46	2.37	2.25	2.05	1.86
Hong Kong	1.39	1.36	1.36	1.22	0.98	0.80
Macau	1.72	1.54	1.40	1.25	1.13	1.02
Mongolia	2.95	2.87	2.74	2.57	2.30	2.03
Republic of Korea	2.00	1.94	1.90	1.78	1.54	1.33
South Asia	2.53	2.65	2.60	2.45	2.24	1.98
Eastern South Asia	2.70	2.71	2.64	2.46	2.25	1.99
Brunei	1.90	1.80	1.70	1.56	1.35	1.30
Burma	2.37	2.38	2.40	2.32	2.18	1.99
Democratic Kampuchea	2.77	2.97	2.96	2.70	2.48	2.25
East Timor	2.13	2.31	2.28	2.18	2.03	1.85
Indonesia[e]	2.60	2.59	2.50	2.27	2.03	1.75
Lao People's Democratic Republic	2.18	2.38	2.33	2.24	2.11	1.93
Malaysia	2.89	2.93	2.77	2.55	2.06	1.72
Philippines	3.34	3.22	3.06	2.84	2.61	2.32
Singapore	1.61	1.61	1.57	1.42	1.12	0.88
Socialist Republic of Vietnam	2.11	2.25	2.32	2.31	2.22	2.03
Former Democratic Republic of Vietnam	2.36	2.45	2.48	2.45	2.35	2.16
Former Republic of South Vietnam	1.81	2.01	2.11	2.13	2.04	1.86
Thailand	3.27	3.23	3.11	2.89	2.63	2.35
Middle South Asia	2.44	2.60	2.55	2.40	2.19	1.93
Afghanistan	2.54	2.67	2.69	2.62	2.52	2.35
Bangladesh	1.71	2.79	2.89	2.79	2.59	2.36

[e]Including West Irian.

Projected Average Annual Rates of Growth by Region and Country, 1970–2000, UN Medium Variant

Region and Country	Percentage					
	1970 – 1975	1975–1980	1980–1985	1985–1990	1990–1995	1995–2000
Middle South Asia (cont'd.)						
Bhutan	2.31	2.47	2.52	2.44	2.44	2.20
India	2.43	2.48	2.40	2.25	2.03	1.77
Iran	2.98	3.13	3.08	2.89	2.64	2.35
Maldives	1.95	2.10	2.15	2.20	2.20	2.20
Nepal	2.25	2.48	2.57	2.51	2.48	2.21
Pakistan	3.09	3.24	3.20	3.02	2.74	2.47
Sikkim	2.00	2.10	2.10	2.20	2.20	2.20
Sri Lanka	2.22	2.01	1.88	1.73	1.53	1.29
Western South Asia						
Bahrain	2.83	2.92	2.92	2.81	2.63	2.36
Cyprus	3.08	3.17	3.18	3.12	2.99	2.74
Democratic Yemen	1.23	1.19	1.11	0.93	0.75	0.60
Gaza Strip[f] (Palestine[g])	2.90	2.99	3.01	2.98	2.87	2.64
Iraq	3.40	3.50	3.50	3.40	3.10	2.90
Israel	3.36	3.44	3.40	3.20	3.01	2.81
Jordan	2.88	2.64	2.26	1.87	1.59	1.41
Kuwait	3.29	3.34	3.32	3.17	3.02	2.82
Lebanon	7.13	5.63	4.66	4.10	3.76	3.36
Oman	3.00	3.16	3.26	3.18	2.95	2.60
Qatar	3.08	3.17	3.18	3.12	2.99	2.74
Saudi Arabia	3.10	3.17	3.18	3.12	2.99	2.74
Syrian Arab Republic	2.94	3.01	3.04	3.00	2.89	2.66
	3.00	3.24	3.33	3.19	3.02	2.81

Turkey	2.48	2.58	2.61	2.53	2.31	1.95
United Arab Emirates	3.08	3.17	3.18	3.12	2.99	2.74
Yemen	2.90	2.99	3.01	2.98	2.87	2.64
Europe	0.60	0.56	0.54	0.54	0.51	0.48
Eastern Europe	0.64	0.63	0.56	0.50	0.48	0.51
Bulgaria	0.70	0.63	0.54	0.49	0.49	0.50
Czecholosvakia	0.62	0.61	0.51	0.44	0.45	0.53
German Democratic Republic[h]	0.08	0.12	0.16	0.19	0.20	0.25
Hungary	0.38	0.35	0.22	0.12	0.12	0.18
Poland	0.83	0.85	0.76	0.61	0.52	0.52
Romania	0.90	0.81	0.76	0.76	0.79	0.79
Northern Europe	0.41	0.43	0.42	0.44	0.44	0.44
Channel I.	0.85	0.80	0.75	0.70	0.65	0.55
Denmark	0.39	0.31	0.26	0.25	0.25	0.22
Faeroe I.	0.71	0.69	0.67	0.55	0.58	0.52
Finland	0.20	0.16	0.09	0.11	0.04	0.01
Iceland	1.15	1.17	1.14	1.04	0.90	0.78
Ireland	1.17	1.04	1.05	1.02	0.94	0.86
Isle of Man	0.77	0.78	0.75	0.66	0.49	0.33
Norway	0.66	0.56	0.49	0.43	0.40	0.37
Sweden	0.61	0.61	0.52	0.47	0.45	0.44
United Kingdom	0.34	0.38	0.40	0.45	0.45	0.46

[f] Comprising that part of Palestine under Egyptian administration following the Armistice of 1949 until June 1967, when it was occupied by Israeli military forces.

[g] Former mandated territory administered by the United Kingdom until the Armistice of 1949.

[h] Including Berlin. Designations and data for Berlin appearing on these pages were supplied by the competent authorities pursuant to the relevant agreements of the Four Powers.

APPENDIX TABLE 2 (Continued)
Projected Average Annual Rates of Growth by Region and Country, 1970–2000, UN Medium Variant

Region and County	Percentage					
	1970–1975	1975–1980	1980–1985	1985–1990	1990–1995	1995–2000
Southern Europe						
Andorra	0.72	0.71	0.68	0.66	0.62	0.57
Albania	3.47	2.34	2.02	1.90	1.79	1.76
Gibraltar	2.70	2.63	2.50	2.22	1.86	1.61
Greece	0.74	0.65	0.56	0.54	0.40	0.39
Holy See	0.31	0.33	0.31	0.32	0.29	0.24
Italy	0.00	0.00	0.00	0.00	0.00	0.00
Malta	0.54	0.47	0.42	0.40	0.38	0.36
Portugal	0.23	0.34	0.27	0.11	−0.09	−0.22
San Marino	0.31	0.44	0.54	0.56	0.51	0.43
Spain	1.02	0.87	0.84	0.80	0.77	0.82
Yugoslavia	0.91	0.90	0.82	0.74	0.65	0.59
Western Europe						
Austria	0.58	0.46	0.48	0.50	0.46	0.40
Belgium	0.24	0.24	0.27	0.32	0.33	0.33
France	0.43	0.43	0.42	0.37	0.31	0.29
Germany, Federal Republic of[h]	0.87	0.81	0.70	0.61	0.57	0.53
Liechtenstein	0.32	0.11	0.27	0.42	0.36	0.27
Luxembourg	1.01	0.88	0.92	0.80	0.85	0.74
Monaco	0.18	0.15	0.14	0.13	0.11	0.10
Netherlands	0.84	0.81	0.70	0.68	0.51	0.43
Switzerland	0.85	0.73	0.71	0.68	0.62	0.53
Oceania	1.96	1.94	1.86	1.73	1.59	1.45

Australia and New Zealand	1.83	1.78	1.66	1.49	1.34	1.24
Australia	1.91	1.84	1.71	1.52	1.34	1.23
New Zealand	1.45	1.47	1.44	1.36	1.30	1.27
Melanesia	2.41	2.57	2.64	2.64	2.50	2.17
New Caledonia	2.84	2.89	2.88	2.79	2.68	2.34
New Hebrides	2.78	2.74	3.01	2.79	2.67	2.35
Norfolk I.	0.00	0.00	0.00	0.00	0.00	0.00
Papua New Guinea	2.36	2.53	2.60	2.62	2.47	2.14
Solomon I.	2.81	2.89	2.88	2.79	2.67	2.35
Micronesia and Polynesia	2.55	2.55	2.45	2.28	2.12	1.86
Micronesia	2.70	2.71	2.59	2.36	2.26	2.06
Gilbert I. & Tuvalu	3.38	2.94	2.59	2.41	2.33	2.08
Guam	2.34	2.69	2.75	2.46	2.30	2.16
Nauru	1.38	1.29	1.21	1.14	1.08	1.03
Niue I.	1.54	1.43	1.33	1.25	1.18	1.11
Pacific I.	2.90	2.86	2.69	2.43	2.34	2.09
Other Micronesiaⁱ	1.45	1.31	1.37	1.36	1.39	1.40
Polynesia	2.50	2.50	2.41	2.26	2.08	1.80
American Samoa	3.13	3.24	3.32	3.09	2.81	2.38
Cook I.	3.11	3.19	3.33	3.11	2.77	2.41
Fiji	2.08	1.91	1.69	1.50	1.37	1.20
French Polynesia	3.12	3.27	3.29	3.09	2.81	2.38
Tonga	3.12	3.27	3.28	3.09	2.80	2.39
Wallis & Futuna I.	0.00	0.00	0.00	0.00	0.00	0.00
Western Samoa	3.13	3.28	3.26	3.09	2.82	2.38
U.S.S.R.	0.99	1.00	0.98	0.85	0.73	0.67

ⁱIncluding Canton and Enderbury Islands, Christmas Island, Cocos (Keeling) Islands, Johnston Island, Midway Islands, Pitcairn Island, Tokelau Islands, and Wake Island.

SOURCE: UN, *World Population Prospects as Assessed in 1973*, pp. 90–97.

Index

About the Authors

GEORGES TAPINOS is Professor of Economics and Demography and a senior research fellow at the Institute of Political Studies in Paris. He is also visiting professor at the University of Louvain, Belgium. International migration, economic demography, and the history of economic thought are his main research interests. Professor Tapinos' publications include *L'Économie des Migrations Internationales*, *L'Immigration Etrangère en France*, *International Migration: Proceedings of a Seminar* (editor), and numerous articles. He received his Doctorat ès Sciences Économiques from the University of Paris (Sorbonne) in 1973, and in 1974 he received his Agrégation de Sciences Économiques. Professor Tapinos has served as a consultant to the UN, OECD, and ILO, among others; he is a member of the Union Internationale pour l'Étude Scientifique de la Population.

PHYLLIS T. PIOTROW is Executive Director of the Population Crisis Committee in Washington, D.C. She previously was the administrator for the Population Information Program at the George Washington University Medical Center and was a consultant to the United Nations Center for Economic and Social Information. Dr. Piotrow was the recipient of a Marshall Fellowship for study at Oxford University and a Ford Fellowship for research in public administration and population at The Johns Hopkins University. Her professional activities include membership in the Population Association of America, in the American Public Health Association, and on the Board of Directors of the Center for Population Activities. She received a B.A. from Bryn Mawr College, a B.A. and M.A. from Oxford, and a Ph.D. in political science and population dynamics from Johns Hopkins. Dr. Piotrow is the author of *World Population Crisis: The United States Response* and several articles on population.

EDWARD L. MORSE is a Special Assistant in the Office of Undersecretary for Economic Affairs, Department of State. He was formerly Executive Director of the 1980s Project at the Council on Foreign Relations.